REVISED

PROCLAIM

HIS

HOLY NAME

UNCOVERING YEHOVAH'S WILL FOR HIS NAME

PETER AND LINDA MILLER-RUSSO

Copyright © 2011, 2014 Peter and Linda Miller-Russo. All rights reserved. No part of this book may be reproduced in any form, stored in a retrieval system, or transmitted in any form by any means—electronic, mechanical, photocopy, recording, or otherwise—without prior written permission of the authors except as provided by United States of America copyright law.

The authors are non-denominational Christian believers who love the Word and wish to honor the Father and the Son by proclaiming Their holy names as revealed in the scriptures. They are not affiliated with any particular group or movement.

Unless otherwise noted all Biblical quotations are taken from the King James version of the Bible. The authors have **bolded** various words in the verses to provide their own emphasis. Italics used by the King James translators have been left as is. At times the authors have added their own explanatory words in brackets [...] within a verse.

Within the verse references the word "G_d" has been replaced by the Hebrew word "Elohim" which means "Mighty One." Upper case "LORD" has been changed to the Father's name which He gave us in the Hebrew scriptures. Other occurrences of "Lord" have been changed to either Father's name or Master as context dictates. The term "Christ" has been changed to "Messiah." Lastly, the actual name of Elohim and His Son's Hebrew name have been given their rightful place within the Bible verses.

Scripture quotations marked as NAS are taken from the NEW AMERICAN STANDARD BIBLE®, Copyright © 1960,1962,1963,1968,1971,1972,

1973,1975,1977,1995 by The Lockman Foundation. Used by permission.

Scripture quotations marked as NLT are taken from the Holy Bible, New Living Translation, copyright ©1996, 2004, 2007 by Tyndale House Foundation. Used by permission of Tyndale House Publishers, Inc., Carol Stream, Illinois 60188. All rights reserved.

Scripture quotations marked GWT are taken from GOD'S WORD®, © 1995 God's Word to the Nations. Used by permission of Baker Publishing Group.

Scriptures quotations marked as YLT are from the Holy Bible, Young's Literal Translation.

Cover Design and Cover Photo © 2011, 2014 Peter and Linda Miller-Russo

Second Edition - Revised and Expanded 01/2014

ISBN 978-0-9833633-0-9

Proclaim His Holy Name **is published by**
Only Believe Publishing, LLC
(www.onlybelievepublishing.com)

For more information on the Father's name visit:
www.ProclaimHisHolyName.org

Dedication

We dedicate this book to our Heavenly Father, our Mighty Elohim, Creator of all that is. We present it to the world with the belief that all who read it with a desire for Elohim in their hearts will come to know, honor, proclaim, and lift-up His Holy Name above all else in this life and in the life to come.

Holy is Your Name Yehovah,
O Heavenly Father,
All light and goodness flow from You.
For You are the Designer, the Builder,
the endless Sustainer of worlds
both known and unknown.

Author and Source of the visible and the invisible,
Holy and Eternal Spirit, Who formed us in the womb,
Who gave us breath.

Holy, majestic, and merciful Father, Divine Healer,
Who binds every wound
And forgives every sin.

Our Mighty One Who searches every heart
and hears our every cry
Who wipes away every tear. Hallelujah!

Contents

	Introduction	1
1	Our Creator wants His Name Proclaimed	7
2	What's in a Name?	25
3	The Name of the Mighty One of Israel	41
4	Who is the Messiah and What is His Name?	63
5	The Fulfillment of the Law	81
6	The Prophecy of Malachi	91
7	Blessings and Curses	101
8	Israel the Chosen	121
9	The Prophecy of Hosea	139
10	Keeping the Name Pure	153
11	Jerusalem—Where the Name has been Placed	167
12	Pure Praise Pure Worship	183
13	The Creator's Will	201
14	Calling on the Name	221
15	Promises in the Messiah's Name	239
16	Your Name in Eternity	271
	How to receive Salvation and Eternal Life	293

APPENDICES

A.	The Creator Proclaimed His own Name	305
B.	Timeline of Elohim	315
C.	Verse References by Type	319
D.	Verse References by Books of the Bible	325
E.	The Attributes of the Creator	331
F.	The Great Deeds of the Creator	333
G.	References	339

Introduction

A Message from Peter

My wife Linda and I had the privilege of traveling to the land of Israel in the fall of 2009. One night, during our stay in the holy city of Jerusalem, I felt compelled to begin writing about the holy name of our Creator. I had only learned that the name of our Creator was not "the LORD" a few short years earlier. Now as I sat in the common room of our Jerusalem hotel the reality that I was in Israel, that I was actually in the very city where His holy name was placed, stirred my spirit deeply. The words of the first chapter of this book flowed out of my fingertips that night but it was only the beginning.

When we returned back home I realized that I needed to know more before the initial chapter could be expanded into a complete work. Thus began the process of cataloging all the verses in the Bible where the word "name" and the name of our Creator appeared. I was surprised by the sheer amount of verses that focus on the Name and its importance and was dismayed by the lack of attention that is actually given to His name in our world—secular *and* religious.

Perhaps the most difficult chapter to complete was the chapter that sought to uncover the actual pronunciation of the name of the Creator. In case you were not aware, there is much debate about this topic. Therefore, Linda and I did extensive research and had many detailed discussions. We asked for insight from the Holy Spirit.

The night that we finally came to a common agreement on the pronunciation of the Name I had an incredible dream of confirmation. In the dream I heard voices singing. The singing was coming from what I sensed was a huge unseen chorus of over 10,000 angels. They were singing the word "Alleluia" (Hallelujah). Their singing seemed to be coming from behind me, but then it felt as if it began to flow through me like a wave. It felt as if my body was being played like a musical instrument. Then, to my amazement I was lifted off the ground by what felt like an energy of all pervading love that had pierced my heart. I was being drawn upwards towards its source. When I awoke I knew that the dream was a sign that Linda and I had made the proper choice regarding the pronunciation of our Creator's holy name.

My strongest hope for you and others that read this work is that the Creator's love also touches your heart and transforms your life like His love is doing in mine. I also hope that the information in this book will spur you to go beyond the man-made rules and traditions that prevent us from understanding who our Creator actually is. Now is the time for all people to honor the Father's desire for His holy name to be known and proclaimed throughout all the nations of the world—starting with *you* and with *me*.

A Message from Linda

Throughout my life I have been reaching out to the Creator in many different ways, trying to draw close to Him. I meditated out in nature; I prayed, I fasted, I wrote letters to Him—but I still wasn't satisfied. I knew that if Elohim was to be found I would need to study His holy Word. Unfortunately I only understood part of what I was reading, and I had difficulty knowing how to apply the Word to my life. But as the Word says, "seek and ye shall find," and I am so honored to be able to say: I found Him. Or I should say, His Holy Spirit found me.

Here is how it happened: One sunny summer day a few years ago I found myself home alone with a whole day all to myself. I took my Bible outside onto our deck, sat down, and began to read the book of Psalms. The words were so beautiful that I felt led to read them out loud, praising the Father with words written by King David over 3000 years ago. Hour after hour went by, and I found that I had no desire to stop reading—the beauty of the praise had a joyous intensity that kept building as I read—like a dance you never want to end. After several hours of reading out loud, I felt something I can only describe as a vibration of LIGHT thrilling through my body, an inner illumination that I knew had to be the spiritual presence of our Creator. It was as if the Creator was in me, and I was in Him. I was experiencing the promise of Psalm 22:3: *"But Thou art holy, O Thou that **inhabitest the praises** of Israel."* As I bathed in His Holy Spirit, I was impressed with the knowledge that Peter and I needed to go to a spiritual conference, to connect with like-minded believers. This resulted in our decision to attend several Christian conferences, where we were baptized in the Holy Spirit and received the gift of speaking in tongues. Since then the "eyes of my understanding" have been opened and the Word has come alive for me. I don't struggle to understand the Bible now—in fact, I have a hard time getting myself to stop reading it, especially at night, right before bed—the Word opens up, and sometimes it is three a.m. before I can get myself to go to sleep.

    This focus on the Word has great rewards. For example, after studying Isaiah chapters 52-58, and meditating on how our Messiah fulfilled these prophesies, I woke up one night from what I can only describe as one of the most beautiful dreams/visions I have ever had. In this vision I saw the words of the

Book of Isaiah and Joel flowing through my mind, being absorbed into my heart, and becoming an actual part of me. Every word was permeated with the love of Elohim, and I knew the Holy Spirit was gifting me with this glimpse into how He works within the hearts of believers. A sense of thankfulness and perfect peace filled me—and then something incredible happened. I suddenly felt a communion host being placed gently upon my tongue, by the heavenly hand of our Saviour! I knew at that moment, beyond a shadow of a doubt, that I was saved, blessed, and will be forever held within the loving arms of our Elohim.

Experiences like these are available to every believer who seeks Elohim with their whole heart. Pursue Him, take time to praise Him and His holy name every day; deepen your relationship with Him by immersing yourself in the Word; call upon Him by name and His Holy Spirit will dwell within you, showing you all things.

I thank you, Heavenly Father, for the dedicated Jewish scribes who throughout history preserved Your holy Word and Your holy name (Tetragrammaton) within the pages of the Tanakh. I thank you also for my many blessings: For my inspired husband Peter; for my insightful daughter Jen; for our beautiful farm; and for all my loved ones called into salvation by Your Holy Spirit through the sacrifice of Your dear Son.

Proclaim His Holy Name

Chapter 1

Our Creator wants His Name Proclaimed

> And in very deed for this *cause* have I raised thee up, for to show *in* thee my power; and that my name may be declared throughout all the earth.
>
> Exodus 9:16

Each week all across the world, followers of Judaism and Christianity gather together in their synagogues and churches to worship the Creator. In an earnest desire to honor the Father and to show the depth of love they have for Him they sing songs of praise to Him and listen to their rabbis, pastors, and priests read from His Word. They humble themselves in His presence and seek His favor for themselves and their loved ones. Each one of them desires to draw closer to their Creator—the One who has formed them in the womb and blessed them with the Spirit of Life.

While most believers desire deeper intimacy with

their Creator, they do not know His true name nor understand the significance of using it. Most people also do not understand what the Creator's will is for His holy name and how this knowledge could bless them. However, this need not be the case as there are more than 300 verses from the Old Testament and over 500 from the entire Bible that proclaim the significance of His name as well as His will for His name. In fact, the Creator Himself states exactly what His name is over 150 times in the Old Testament alone. For example:

> I *am* the LORD: that *is* my name: and my glory will I not give to another, neither my praise to graven images.
>
> ISAIAH 42:8

You may ask "where is the name of the Creator, the Mighty One of Israel, in this verse?" It is hidden in the phrase "the LORD." The phrase or title "the LORD" was substituted for the actual name of the Creator during translation from the original Hebrew text. The title "the LORD" is not the Creator's name. The Creator's name is found in four Hebrew letters יהוה pronounced as "Yod-Hey-Vav-Hey (YHVH)." These four letters (His holy name) are written over 6820 times[1] in the Hebrew Bible (the Christian's "Old" Testament) and are called the Tetragrammaton (from the Greek meaning four letters).

Yet, because of a non-scriptural tradition instituted centuries ago which states that the name of the Creator is too holy to speak, whenever an observant Jew reading Hebrew scripture comes to the name of the Mighty One he/she will substitute another word or the phrase "Ha Shem" (the Name).

Most Christian Bible translators followed this tradition by replacing the true Name as found in the Hebrew scriptures with the non-descript title of "the lord"—the title given to an owner of land (landlord). However they did distinguish it by capitalizing the word as LORD in most English translations of the Bible. Other Bible translations have changed the Name to "the Lord" with only the "L" capitalized. While this also hides the name of the Creator, it creates even more problems as it blurs the line between the Father and the Son since the Son is referred to as "Lord" with a capital "L" in the New Testament.

But isn't it better to show the Creator our love for Him by following His will and direction regarding His holy name rather than following the traditions of men? And what is Elohim's will regarding His name? It is for His name to be declared (proclaimed) to all mankind throughout the world. This is shown in the verse at the start of this chapter (Exodus 9:16) and it will be clearly shown from many other scriptures throughout the pages of this book.

What does it mean to proclaim His name? To proclaim means *"to publicly announce," "to declare," "to publish,"* and *"to make widely known."* Yet, even though scripture tells us that the Mighty One of the Jews and the Christians desires His name to be proclaimed, most Christians have never been taught His true name and therefore cannot proclaim it while most religious Jews, while aware of His name, will not say it out loud.

We do not believe that the lack of awareness of the actual name of the Father (as well as the lack of knowledge regarding His will for His name) is the fault of sincere believers. It is actually not even the fault of the rabbis and pastors who lead the people. Rather, it is Satan, the father of all lies, who has blinded man's eyes to the glorious name and will of the Father.

However, the Messiah, through his sacrifice on the cross, has overcome the world and defeated Satan once and for all. Therefore, the responsibility to break this tradition of men which hides the name of the Creator and thwarts His will on Earth belongs to us and to our spiritual leaders. The time has come for us to light our lamps and to know the Father by name as He knows us by name:

And the LORD said unto Moses, I will do

> this thing also that thou hast spoken: for thou hast found grace in my sight, and I know thee by name.
>
> EXODUS 33:17

Scripture Reveals, Tradition Blinds

Most people believe that the Ten Commandments were first given on tablets of stone as shown in the movie, 'The Ten Commandments.' This is not accurate. Scripture reveals in the book of Exodus that the Ten Commandments were actually first *spoken* down from the top of Mount Sinai to the nation of Israel audibly by the Father Himself. He began with:

> I *am* the LORD thy G_d, which have brought thee out of the land of Egypt, out of the house of bondage. Thou shalt have no other g_ds before me.
>
> EXODUS 20:2-3

In breaking down this instruction we find in the original Hebrew that:

1. YHVH identified Himself

YHVH first made sure that the Israelites knew His name—and He didn't say "the LORD."

2. YHVH stated what He had done for them

YHVH made sure that they knew it was He who redeemed them from slavery.

3. YHVH taught the people

YHVH lastly stated the actual instruction to the people: that other g_ds (elohim / mighty ones) should not be placed before Him.

To illustrate the importance of the Name of the Father consider if the verse was written as follows:

> I am your G_d, which have brought thee out of the land of Egypt, out of the house of bondage. Thou shalt have no other mighty ones before me.

OR simply:

> Thou shalt have no other mighty ones before me.

The Father did not hide His name. It was the FIRST thing He ever spoke audibly to the nation of Israel. If YHVH had hidden His name and not proclaimed it as the example verses above state, then how would the people know whom they should follow? In other words, "thou shalt have no other mighty ones before **who**?"

Imagine that you are standing in front of a flagpole with your eyes closed. You can hear a flag flying in the wind. The person next to you asks, "Will you pledge allegiance to this flag?" What will you answer? You will most likely answer that you can't pledge allegiance to the flag until you open your eyes and identify which country the flag stands for. You can't give your oath to defend that country and to live under its rules until you know which country it is. To do so would be foolishness. Similarly, how can you give allegiance to an elohim (g_d) whose name or values you do not know?

Top Five Names in the Bible by count

Rank	Name	Meaning	Count
1	YHVH	Who shall be, who is, who was	6948
2	David	Beloved	1064
3	Jesus	YHVH is salvation	984
4	Moses	Drawn out of water	847
5	Jacob	The Supplanter	377

As you can see from the chart above scripture has clearly revealed the Father's name to us. Scripture also clearly shows that He wants it proclaimed throughout the Earth but Satan has influenced men into creating traditions that hinder the Word and Will of YHVH rather than advancing it; traditions that say the Name of YHVH is too holy to utter and that replace His name with the title "the LORD." Satan's plan has placed the Father's name in a hazy fog thus making the Name of none-effect. This is evident in the fact that most of mankind believes that even though different world religions have different names for the Creator they nevertheless all worship the same Being.

THIS IS **NOT** TRUE

All World religions do NOT worship the same G_d!

In the New Testament passage of Jesus with the woman at the well of Jacob in Samaria Jesus told the Samaritan woman that they (the Samaritans) did not know what they worshipped and that salvation is 'of the Jews' (John 4:22). Therefore, if someone is not following the Elohim of Abraham, Isaac, and Jacob, the Elohim of Israel, the Father of Yehoshua (Jesus) and His plan of redemption through the blood sacrifice of His Son then they are following the father of all lies, Satan. The **only** way to the Father is through a Jew whom we call Jesus:

> Jesus saith unto him, I am the way, the truth, and the life: no man cometh unto the Father, but by me.
>
> JOHN 14:6

And who is Jesus' Father? It's not the name of any other g_d of any other world religion. Jesus' Father is יהוה (YHVH)—the name that is written over 6800 times in the Hebrew scriptures (which are the original source of Christian Bible translations).

Yet translations such as the Amplified Bible show that, in addition to changing the Father's name to a title, *the editors didn't even understand that His name is **not** that title.* For example, the editors revealed how Satan had blinded them when they wrote the following footnote on Genesis 18:14:

> The word "Lord" as applied to God is obviously the most important word in the Bible, for it occurs oftener than any other important word—by actual count more than 5,000 times. **Nothing** is "too hard *or* too wonderful" for Him when He is truly made Lord.
>
> GENESIS CHAPTER 18, FOOTNOTE "J" (AMP)

If one examines the original Hebrew text of Genesis 18:14 they will find that the Father's name does not equate to the English word 'Lord' or even the Hebrew word 'Adonai.' The verse actually contains the four Hebrew letters of the Father's name (YHVH). This example is not given to criticize the editors of the Amplified Bible which has many good points. It is given to show just how blind we've become regarding the Father's name.

Just what does this tradition of blindness regarding the Father's name enable Satan to do? It enables him to deceive man into accepting a One-World Religion and a One-World Government. Satan's plan to overthrow the Creator relies upon these two pillars. The anti-Christ shall use these two institutions to control the world and to fight the last battle against the Creator and those loyal to the Heavenly Father.

A liar from the beginning, Satan is again attempting to trick people, this time into believing that all religions worship and honor the same G_d and that all paths lead to Heaven. We can see the plan unfolding with modern day apostasies such as the "interfaith" movement, "new age" Christianity, as well as the attempt to blend Christianity and Islam, aka "Chrislam" under the guise of peace and unity. If people are led to believe that all religions worship the same Creator then the salvation that comes from 'the Jews' as Jesus taught will be lost and the unfortunate deceived will be led down the wide path that leads to destruction in hell.

How about you? Are you ready to consider and follow what the Word says rather than follow traditions created by religious establishments? Will you seek the will and wisdom of our heavenly Father?

> Wisdom *is* the principal thing; *therefore* get wisdom: and with all thy getting get understanding.
> PROVERBS 4:7

The following is a partial list of what you will learn as you read this book and meditate on the scripture verses included throughout its pages:

- ✻ The true name of the Creator
- ✻ How to pronounce His name
- ✻ How to honor His name
- ✻ What the Creator desires for His name
- ✻ The true name of the Messiah—the Son of Elohim
- ✻ The many promises in the Messiah's name
- ✻ How to receive blessings in the Father's name for yourself and your loved ones
- ✻ How to ensure that your name and your

loved ones names are found in the "Book of Life"

✹ How to have a personal page in the Father's "Book of Remembrance"

Thou Shalt not Add nor Diminish

While the omission of the holy name of the Creator from our vocabulary is nearly universal, other pagan terms used to address the Creator have infected our languages and are replacements for His name that do not please Him. Just as in the original covenant times when the Creator commanded the children of Israel to completely eradicate His enemies from the lands that He had given to Jacob's seed, we should eradicate words from our lexicon that give glory to other "mighty" ones. As the Word says, there is no one that is good except the Father in Heaven (Mark 10:18). Therefore it is to Him, to His name, that all the glory, honor, and praise is due.

> Because I will publish [proclaim] the name of the LORD: ascribe ye greatness unto our Elohim.
>
> DEUTERONOMY 32:3

We have been given many commands from the Father—all for our benefit. According to Rabbinic sources, the Torah (the first five books of the Bible) contains 613 commandments. Some only pertain to priests (Levites), some to women, some only to men. In Deuteronomy 4:2 Moses warns us not to add or to take away from the Creator's commandments:

> Ye shall not add unto the word which I command you, neither shall ye diminish *ought* from it, that ye may keep the commandments of the LORD your Elohim which I command you.
> DEUTERONOMY 4:2

However, contrary to the instructions in Deuteronomy 4:2 rabbinic leaders have added man-made laws that are not part of the Creator's commands. For example, the rule for the ceremonial washing of one's hands before meals was added as a new commandment in the written and oral traditions of the rabbis. It is not found in the Torah. Other non-scriptural commands that the rabbis added range from which shoe to tie first to how far one can walk on the Sabbath day.

The historic Church is also guilty of adding new commandments, such as restrictions on eating meat on Friday and rulings that only members of their denomination may partake of the Saviour's communion. They also took away (diminished) from the commandments by changing the day of the Sabbath to Sunday. This practice of adding and removing commandments has resulted in the tradition of translating the Creator's name into "the LORD." It has blinded us to the Father's will regarding His holy name.

Thus, in spite of the scriptural evidence that the Creator wants us to proclaim His name to the world, most people have taken a seat at the table of the traditions of men; some because it feels more comfortable and others from a misunderstanding and therefore misapplication of the scriptures to their daily life. As the Messiah said:

> Enter ye in at the strait [narrow] gate: for wide *is* the gate, and broad *is* the way, that leadeth to destruction, and many there be which go in thereat:
> MATTHEW 7:13

The Messiah never sinned. He followed all of the Creator's commandments. In fact, he taught us Elohim's true intent—for not only must we follow the *letter* of the Law, we must also adhere to the *spirit* of the Law:

> Ye have heard that it was said by them of old time, Thou shalt not commit adultery: But I say unto you, That whosoever looketh on a woman to lust after her hath committed adultery with her already in his heart.
> MATTHEW 5:27-28

How can anyone who loves the Creator and believes in His Word continue to choose to follow the traditions of men—especially traditions that do not honor the Father's will? The Messiah reprimanded the religious leaders of his day in Mark 7:13:

> Making the word of Elohim of none effect through your tradition, which ye have delivered: and many such like things do ye.
> MARK 7:13

By changing the true name of the Creator, as found in the original Hebrew text, the religious translators have, in actuality, made the name of Elohim of none effect! This man-made tradition continues up to this very day. There are few people in the world who know Elohim's name. They sing songs to His name without singing His name—as if the word "name" is actually the Creator's name. Thus, a nameless Creator has been and continues to be presented to the world by rabbis, pastors, and priests whose duty it is to lead the world to Him. Instead, tricked by the devil, they have given the world a placeholder—a blank title "the LORD" (a man-made tradition). How does this show honor and respect for the Father's name? And what could be the reward for those who place the traditions of men above the Word of the Creator?

> And then will I profess unto them, I never knew you: depart from me, ye that work iniquity.
>
> MATTHEW 7:23

The Greek word "anomian" translated as "*iniquity*" above has another meaning: "*lawlessness.*" Lawlessness is not following the Father's will. If one reads the verses surrounding Matthew 7:23, they will find that the Messiah is explaining that not all those who claim to perform works in his name will enter the kingdom of Heaven—but only those who do the will of his Father. Part of the will of the Father, as we will show through the scriptural references included in this book, is to glorify and proclaim His holy name to all.

Let us choose to follow the Father's will not out of blind obedience, but out of a genuine desire to have a deeper relationship with Him.

Our Creator Wants His Name Proclaimed

I will extol thee, my Elohim, O King; and I will bless thy name for ever and ever. Every day will I bless thee; and I will praise thy name for ever and ever. Great *is* the LORD, and greatly to be praised; and his greatness *is* unsearchable.

PSALMS 145:1-3

Proclaim His Holy Name

Chapter 2

WHAT'S IN A NAME?

> A *good* name *is* rather to be chosen than great riches, *and* loving favor rather than silver and gold.
>
> PROVERBS 22:1

Why is the Creator's name so important to Him? To understand this, let's take a look at what's in a name.

First of all, a name does much more than identify you to others. It embodies your character, your personality, and your reputation. While your last name connects you to the past (all the way back to Adam and Eve in fact), your first name is so closely intertwined with you in the present that the misuse of it can elicit strong emotions. For example, have you ever had the experience in grade school of being teased by others using your name? Peter's was "Peter Peter Pumpkin Eater." On the other hand, did you ever get positive remarks from your teacher who mentioned you by name, and how well you did on a particular task? Most of us have experienced both.

Those of you who are parents went through the task of choosing a name for your child. This process for most people is not a quick one. They search through baby name books trying to find the one perfect name that just "fits." Somehow we instinctively know that the name we give our child is the first significant choice that can have a positive impact on the rest of his/her life.

While some parents choose a name because they like the sound of it, others place a greater importance upon a name's meaning. The following tables display the top baby names in the U.S.A. over a period of ten years (2000-2010) along with their meanings and language of origin. It's interesting to note that six of the ten names (and all of the male names) are derived from the Hebrew language—the language of the Creator:

Boy's names*

Rank	Name	Meaning	Origin
1	Jacob	The Supplanter	Hebrew
2	Michael	Who is like Elohim	Hebrew
3	Joshua	Elohim is Salvation	Hebrew
4	Matthew	Gift of Elohim	Hebrew
5	Daniel	Elohim is my Judge	Hebrew

* Based on U.S. Social Security applications Jan. 2000 - Feb. 2010

Girl's names*

Rank	Name	Meaning	Origin
1	Emily	Eager	Latin
2	Madison	Son of the mighty one	English
3	Emma	All embracing	German
4	Olivia	Olive Tree	Latin
5	Hannah	Elohim has favored me	Hebrew

* Based on U.S. Social Security applications Jan. 2000 - Feb. 2010

The Creator, the Father of all, named the first human being Adam. The name Adam comes from the Hebrew word "adama" which means "*earth.*" The Creator then gave Adam the privilege of naming all the creatures on the Earth:

> And out of the ground the LORD Elohim formed every beast of the field, and every fowl of the air; and brought *them* unto Adam to see what he would call them: and whatsoever Adam called every living creature, that *was* the name thereof.
> GENESIS 2:19

The Creator also gave new names to Biblical personalities that had or were about to experience a transition. The newly given name more closely matched the person's current purpose in life. In the following verse the Creator renames Abram to Abraham:

> Neither shall thy name any more be called Abram, but thy name shall be Abraham; for a father of many nations have I made thee.
>
> GENESIS 17:5

Abraham's original name "Abram" means "*exalted father.*" The new name he was given by the Creator means "*father of many.*" The difference may appear to be slight but Abraham's new name more accurately reflected his new anointing. This shows how much care and emphasis the Creator places on names. Elohim goes on to promise Abraham that He would make Abraham's name great—note that this is a *promise* not a curse, in other words, having a great name was of very high value:

> And I will make of thee a great nation, and I will bless thee, and **make thy name great**; and thou shalt be a blessing:
>
> GENESIS 12:2

The Creator did not stop the changing of names with Abraham; He also gave Abraham's wife Sarai a new name:

What's in a Name?

> And Elohim said unto Abraham, as for Sarai thy wife, thou shalt not call her name Sarai, but Sarah *shall* her name *be*.
>
> GENESIS 17:15

Once again the difference in names is slight but exact. The meaning of "Sarai" is "*my princess*" and the meaning of "Sarah" is simply "*princess.*" Sarah received her new name when she was healed of her infertility. She changed from being Abraham's princess to a princess of her family and tribe.

Continuing to show the importance of naming, the Creator proclaimed that Sarah's son would be named Isaac:

> And Elohim said, Sarah thy wife shall bear thee a son indeed; and thou shalt call his name Isaac: and I will establish my covenant with him for an everlasting covenant, *and* with his seed after him.
>
> GENESIS 17:19

Isaac means "*may Elohim smile*" or "*laughter.*" Perhaps this name was given to Sarah's only natural son because of her reaction when she heard, that as a woman of 95 years of age, she would conceive and bear a child. In the following verse the Creator shows that nothing is impossible for Him to accomplish:

> And the LORD said unto Abraham, Wherefore did Sarah laugh, saying, Shall I of a surety bear a child, which am old? Is any thing too hard for the LORD? At the time appointed I will return unto thee, according to the time of life, and Sarah shall have a son.
> GENESIS 18:13-14

Just as the Creator had declared in Genesis 18:13-14, a son was born to Abraham and Sarah. His name was indeed Isaac and he grew into a great man like his father. When he was 40 years old Isaac married Rebecca and he went on to have two sons (twins) named Esau and Jacob. When Isaac's son Jacob was an adult the Creator continued with the practice of renaming by giving Jacob a new name:

> And Elohim said unto him, thy name *is* Jacob: thy name shall not be called any more Jacob, but Israel shall be thy name: and he called his name Israel.
> GENESIS 35:10

The name Jacob means *"he who follows upon the*

heels of one." This is a reference to the fact that Jacob was actually the second born of twins. Jacob's new name "Israel" means *"he who has striven with Elohim,"* and is directly related to the fact that Jacob wrestled all night with the Creator (Genesis 32:30).

Some believe that only the Creator has the power to change a name, however the children of Israel followed the Creator's example as shown in the following verse where Moses changed the name of Oshea (Joshua) to *Jehoshua*:

> These *are* the names of the men which Moses sent to spy out the land. And Moses called Oshea the son of Nun Jehoshua.
>
> NUMBERS 13:16

The name Oshea means *"salvation."* The new name given by Moses added part of the Creator's name to Oshea's name to make the new name Jehoshua, meaning *"the Creator is salvation."* The meaning of Oshea's new name has even more significance as will be shown in a later chapter.

This pattern of renaming is also found in the new covenant. The Messiah himself renamed some of his disciples:

> And he brought him to Jesus. And when

> Jesus beheld him, he said, Thou art Simon the son of Jona: thou shalt be called Cephas, which is by interpretation, A stone.
>
> JOHN 1:42

"Simon" means *"he has heard."* The new name "Cephas" (Peter in English) means *"rock"* which some interpret as *"hollow rock."* Later in Matthew 16:16-18 the Messiah, as he responds to Peter, states that upon "this rock" he will build his church. There is a debate as to whether the Messiah is stating that upon *Peter* will the church be built, or that the church will be built upon the *revelation* that Peter had regarding the Messiah's identity as the Son of Elohim. Based on other verses it appears that the latter is more likely (Matthew 3:17, Luke 9:35, Acts 4:11-12).

Another renaming event found in the new covenant is not directly apparent unless you compare two of the Gospel accounts side by side:

> and passing by, he saw Levi of Alpheus sitting at the tax-office, and saith to him, 'Be following me,' and he, having risen, did follow him.
>
> MARK 2:14 (YLT)

What's in a Name?

> And Jesus passing by thence, saw a man sitting at the tax-office, named Matthew, and saith to him, 'Be following me,' and he, having risen, did follow him.
>
> MATTHEW 9:9 (YLT)

Levi's name was changed to Matthew as the Messiah called him into service as one of his key disciples who would later write one of the four Gospels. Levi means *"joined in harmony."* His new name Matthew means *"gift of Elohim."*

Even though the Creator has renamed people, and the Messiah has renamed people, and the children of Israel have renamed people; the name of the Creator will never change. In Exodus 3:15 the Creator tells Moses to proclaim His holy name to the children of Israel and states "this *is* my name **for ever**." The name of the Creator will be explored in detail in the next chapter.

Here are three more examples found in the Torah that further show the emphasis on a person's name. In each of the verses it is clear that the family name was to be highly regarded:

> Why should the name of our father be done away from among his family, because he hath no son? Give unto us *therefore* a pos-

> session among the brethren of our father.
> NUMBERS 27:4

> And it shall be, *that* the firstborn which she beareth shall succeed in the name of his brother *which is* dead, that his name be not put out of Israel.
> DEUTERONOMY 25:6

> And Aaron shall bear the names of the children of Israel in the breastplate of judgment upon his heart, when he goeth in unto the holy *place*, for a memorial before the LORD continually.
> EXODUS 28:29

In contrast to the verses that show the importance of keeping the family name intact are two verses below that refer to the destruction of one's name:

> But the LORD thy Elohim shall deliver them unto thee, and shall destroy them with a mighty destruction, until they be destroyed. And he shall deliver their kings into thine hand, and thou shalt **destroy their name** from under heaven: there shall

no man be able to stand before thee, until thou have destroyed them.
DEUTERONOMY 7:23-24

The LORD will not spare him, but then the anger of the LORD and his jealousy shall smoke against that man, and all the curses that are written in this book shall lie upon him, and the LORD shall **blot out his name** from under heaven.
DEUTERONOMY 29:20

It would seem to most of us that it would be enough for the Creator to simply destroy His enemies, yet the Creator shows that the *elimination of the name* of His enemies is as important as the destruction of their bodies.

The Creator values His name and His reputation. He put them both on the line when He proclaimed that He had chosen the nation of Israel to be a special nation—set apart to Him as a nation of priests. The children of Israel agreed to this responsibility at the base of Mount Sinai shortly before the Creator spoke down the ten commandments:

> And ye shall be unto me a kingdom of priests, and an holy nation. These *are* the

> words which thou shalt speak unto the children of Israel. And Moses came and called for the elders of the people, and laid before their faces all these words which the LORD commanded him. And all the people answered together, and said, All that the LORD hath spoken we will do. And Moses returned the words of the people unto the LORD.
>
> EXODUS 19:6-8

When Israel went against the Creator's Torah, which they seemed to do periodically, it reflected poorly upon Elohim's name to the Gentiles—the opposite of the Creator's desire. If you've ever been associated with another person whose decisions affected your reputation you'd have a good idea of how the Creator must have felt when He viewed their transgressions. This is apparent by the following verses in Exodus where Moses advocates for the children of Israel who had grievously sinned by creating and worshipping a golden calf. Moses reminded the Creator of His covenant with the children of Israel and what the world would say if He carried out His desire to destroy them:

> And Moses besought the LORD his Elohim, and said, LORD, why doth thy wrath

wax hot against thy people, which thou hast brought forth out of the land of Egypt with great power, and with a mighty hand? Wherefore should the Egyptians speak, and say, For mischief did he bring them out, to slay them in the mountains, and to consume them from the face of the earth? Turn from thy fierce wrath, and repent of this evil against thy people. Remember Abraham, Isaac, and Israel, thy servants, to whom thou swarest by thine own self, and saidst unto them, I will multiply your seed as the stars of heaven, and all this land that I have spoken of will I give unto your seed, and they shall inherit *it* for ever. And the LORD repented of the evil which he thought to do unto his people.

EXODUS 32:11-14

A Good Name

We have inherited from our Creator (in a manner of speaking) the desire for our name to be respected. We work hard to create and maintain a positive reputation—which is connected directly to our name—through our agreements, actions, and interactions with others. Once a reputation is spoiled it can be very difficult to recover. In some cultures a "loss of face" or reputation leads to ruin. So it's not difficult to understand the importance of a good name. The wisdom of the Word states:

> A good name *is* better than precious ointment; and the day of death than the day of one's birth.
>
> ECCLESIASTES 7:1

What does the Word state about the Creator's name and how important it is to Him? What does He, Himself, want for His name... for His *name*, not a *title* or a *term* that describes Him, but for His *name*? Consider these verses from Exodus:

> And the LORD said unto Moses, Rise up early in the morning, and stand before Pharaoh, and say unto him, Thus saith the LORD Elohim of the Hebrews, Let my people go, that they may serve me. For I will at this time send all my plagues upon thine heart, and upon thy servants, and upon thy people; that thou mayest know that *there is* none like me in all the earth. For now I will stretch out my hand, that I may smite thee and thy people with pestilence; and

> thou shalt be cut off from the earth. And in very deed for this *cause* have I raised thee up, for to shew *in* thee my power; and that **my name may be declared throughout all the earth**.
>
> Exodus 9:13-16

The Creator instructed Moses to deliver a stern message to Pharaoh that it was Elohim's power as the Creator, and not that of any Egyptian deity, which brought Pharaoh and Egypt to the position of superpower of the world. Furthermore, the purpose of the power that Egypt was allowed to wield was given to them in order to demonstrate to the whole world not the greatness of an unknown name, but rather the greatness of the Creator's name:

> Nevertheless he [Elohim] saved them for his **name's** sake, that he might make his mighty **power** to be known.
>
> Psalms 106:8

It is clear from the verses above that the Creator values His name highly. It is also clear that He doesn't want His name hidden but rather He desires that the whole world should know His holy name. Therefore, let us all embrace the Name of our Heavenly Father and lift it up in praise and worship. Let us honor His holy name and boldly declare it every day of our lives as King David teaches us:

> Praise ye the LORD. Praise, O ye servants of the LORD, praise the name of the LORD. Blessed be the name of the LORD from this time forth and for evermore. From the rising of the sun unto the going down of the same the LORD'S name is to be praised.
>
> PSALMS 113:1-3

Chapter 3

THE NAME OF THE MIGHTY ONE OF ISRAEL

> And Moses said unto Elohim, Behold, *when* I come unto the children of Israel, and shall say unto them, The Elohim of your fathers hath sent me unto you; and they shall say to me, What *is* his name? what shall I say unto them?
>
> EXODUS 3:13

The Mighty One of Israel is the Creator of the entire universe. He created the planets, the stars, the heavens, the earth, the angels, and you and I. He is the Elohim (mighty one) that existed before the beginning of time and without whom none of us would be here today. Therefore, He is not only the Mighty One of Israel, He is also the Mighty One of all nations and all peoples of the Earth. He is also the Elohim of the Bible who commands us to have no other mighty ones before Him.

Proclaim His Holy Name

The Creator's name is specifically written down thousands of times in the oldest consistently and accurately transcribed document in the world: the Hebrew Tanakh (Old Testament). The Tanakh is a divinely inspired document that binds together Christians and Jews for it is a book about the same Father that both faiths call their own. Yet as seen in the next verse, Elohim's true name was obscured by Bible translators:

> And Elohim said moreover unto Moses, Thus shalt thou say unto the children of Israel, The LORD Elohim of your fathers, the Elohim of Abraham, the Elohim of Isaac, and the Elohim of Jacob, hath sent me unto you: this *is* my name for ever, and this *is* my memorial unto all generations.
>
> EXODUS 3:15

How does the English translation of Exodus 3:15 obscure the Name? It does so by changing the original four Hebrew letters יהוה (read right to left as YHVH—pronounced Yod, Hey, Vav, Hey) into "the LORD." These four letters do not mean "the LORD" in Hebrew, they are instead the ACTUAL name of the Creator of all things. Rather than changing the Name to a title, the Bible translators should have used a transliteration (spelling a word in a particular language to have the *same* sound as the word in the original language) of the Name. For example if a Mr. Green were to go to France his name would not be changed to Mr. Vert (the word for green in French is vert). Mr. Green's name would still be Mr. Green no matter where is the world he would travel. The Father's name is His name forever and should not be pronounced differently in different languages nor hidden or replaced by mere titles.

This hiding of the true Name is not only found in Exodus 3:15. The four Hebrew letters יהוה appear over 6800 times in the Hebrew Tanakh and they are translated as "the LORD" or a derivative in nearly all versions of the Christian Bible. Additionally, Moses himself did not write the name of the Creator over 1650 times in the Torah so that it could be hidden. He wrote the name over and over to honor the Creator as Exodus 3:15 commands: "this *is* my name **for ever**, and this *is* my memorial unto all generations."

When we correct the mistranslation in Exodus 3:15 by using the actual name of the Creator, the verse reads as follows:

> And Elohim said moreover unto Moses, Thus shalt thou say unto the children of Israel, יהוה [YHVH], Elohim of your fathers, the Elohim of Abraham, the Elohim of Isaac, and the Elohim of Jacob, hath sent

Proclaim His Holy Name

> me unto you: this *is* my name for ever, and this *is* my memorial unto all generations.
>
> EXODUS 3:15

Replacing the name of someone with a title as the Biblical translators did when they changed the Creator's name to "the LORD" just doesn't make sense. If we would do this in our day-to-day life then:

- Instead of the nightly introduction of "Here's Johnny" we'd have heard: "Here's the host."

- At the Academy Awards ceremony when the Best Actor award is announced we would hear: "And the winner of the Best Actor award is: The Actor!"

- When news coverage of the presidential election is ready to announce the winner of the election we would hear: "The next President of the United States is: The President."

Yet as absurd as this sounds, this is just what has happened within the vast majority of Biblical translations. Unfortunately, most Bible readers don't even recognize that the precious name of their Creator has been substituted with a mere title.

Fill-in the Blank:

> Therefore, behold, I will this once cause them to know, I will cause them to know mine hand and my might; and they shall know that my name *is* _____.
>
> JEREMIAH 16:21

What is the correct word for the blank "they shall know that My name is _____?"

- a). the Host
- b). the Actor
- c). the President
- d). the LORD
- e). none of the above

If you answered "e," you are correct. The name of the Creator is יהוה (YHVH).

The following chart displays the name of the Creator in the ancient Paleo-Hebrew text, modern Hebrew text, the English letter equivalents, the sound of the Hebrew letters (transliteration), and the common English translation. Note: Hebrew is always read right to left.

	←——Read right to left			
Ancient Paleo-Hebrew	ꓭ	Y	ꓭ	Z
Modern Hebrew	ה	ו	ה	י
English	H	V	H	Y
Hebrew Letter Name	Hey	Vav	Hey	Yod
Common English Translation	D	R	O	L

Now that we have shown how the name of the Creator is written, we need to determine how it is pronounced. In most languages this would not pose a serious issue. However, the written Hebrew language does not contain any vowels (a,e,i,o,u)—only consonants. Even though vowel markings were added between the 7th and 9th century A.D. by the Masoretes (Jewish scribes from the Karaite sect) there is much disagreement regarding the true pronunciation of the name of YHVH. Many argue, in fact, that the Name should not be uttered since the correct pronunciation is supposedly unknown. However, that would be like a father telling his young son who is learning to talk to shut his mouth since he did not pronounce the word "Daddy" perfectly the first time.

Examining the Clues

In determining the correct pronunciation of the Name we can look at various clues that will help us eliminate words that are unlikely to be correct as well as clues that will help us identify the more probable candidates. The first clue involves the letter "J."

Since the letter "J" and its sound does not exist in the Hebrew language, and did not even appear in the English language until the 1500's, the name that some use for the Creator—Jehovah—is highly unlikely to be the proper pronunciation of YHVH. In other words when the High Priest performed the required ceremony in the Holy of Holies at the Temple on Yom Kippur he did not say the word "Jehovah" because he did not speak any words with the "J" sound. This is not meant to disrespect those who use this name for the Creator however we believe that "Jehovah" can safely be removed from the list of probable pronunciations for the Name.

The next clue in uncovering the proper pronunciation of the Name is found by examining an English verse and its Hebrew original:

> Sing unto Elohim, sing praises to his name: extol him that rideth upon the heavens by

his name JAH, and rejoice before him.

PSALMS 68:4

In Psalms 68:4 the short form of the Creator's name appears to be translated into English as JAH. As we've just discussed however, there is no "J" sound in the Hebrew language—so the translation is incorrect. The original Hebrew letters translated to JAH are Yod and Hey (YH). Dropping the "J" sound and replacing with the "Y" sound from YH the short name of the Creator is YAH. In fact, transliterated Hebrew to English Bibles translate the Hebrew as YAH not JAH.

Another important clue is found in the Hebrew word הללי ה, that most of us know as "hallelujah." הללי ה is translated as "Praise ye the LORD" in most English Bibles:

> Praise ye the LORD [Hallelujah]. O give thanks unto the LORD; for *he is* good: for his mercy *endureth* for ever.
>
> PSALMS 106:1

The Hebrew text translated as "Praise ye the LORD" (HLLYH) is shown broken down from ancient Hebrew (Paleo-Hebrew) into modern Hebrew and then into English in the following table:

The Name of the Mighty One of Israel

← ——— Read right to left

Paleo-Hebrew	ᗺ	⇂	ᄂ	ᄂ	ᗺ
Modern Hebrew	ה	י	ל	ל	ה
English	H	Y	L	L	H
Hebrew Letter Name	Hey	Yod	Lamed	Lamed	Hey
Common English Translation	LORD	the	ye		Praise

When the vowel markings are factored into the Hebrew word הלליה, HLLYH becomes Hal-lu-yah which in English is written as 'Hallelujah' (notice the "y" sound is swapped with the "j" sound when spoken in English). Since we know that the "j" sound doesn't exist in the Hebrew language the actual pronunciation of the last syllable is "YAH." "Praise ye the LORD" is actually "Praise ye YHVH" or in Hebrew "hal-lu-YAH" where YAH is the short form of the Creator's true name.

We could stop here, and like a child learning to speak, we could use the shortened name of YAH and be accurately referring to our Father. However, even as a child's speech progresses, we too will attempt to uncover the full pronunciation of the Name by first assuming that YAH is a prefix (created from the first two letters of **YH**VH) and then examining the remaining two letters of the Tetragrammaton; Vav and Hey.

49

Proclaim His Holy Name

If we take the remaining two letters (Vav and Hey) and review the five possible vowel combinations (a,e,i,o,u), we find the following syllables: vah, veh, vih, voh, and vuh. However, since some linguists consider the "V" in Hebrew to be interchangeable with the "W" then we actually have five additional syllables to consider: wah, weh, wih, woh, and wuh.

The next step is to take the ten syllables above and prefix them with YAH to determine the full name, e.g., YAH-vah, YAH-veh, YAH-wah, YAH-weh. Although logical this would be an incorrect action because in the Biblical Hebrew the letter Hey is never left without a vowel sound to connect two syllables (in our case Yod-Hey + Vav-Hey)[1]. Therefore, the actual correct step is to take the first syllable YAH along with the ten possibilities above and use a vowel to connect them as in Yah-a-vah or Yah-e-vah, etc.

Taking the "H" from YAH and each vowel sound together with the 10 fragments above we get the following possible 50 two-syllable endings:

Set 1:
Havah, Haveh, Havih, Havoh Havuh
Hevah, Heveh, Hevih, Hevoh, Hevuh
Hivah, Hiveh, Hivih, Hivoh, Hivuh
Hovah, Hoveh, Hovih, Hovoh, Hovuh
Huvah, Huveh, Huvih, Huvoh, Huvuh

Set 2:
H_awah, H_aweh, H_awih, H_awoh, H_awuh
H_ewah, H_eweh, H_ewih, H_ewoh, H_ewuh
H_iwah, H_iweh, H_iwih, H_iwoh, H_iwuh
H_owah, H_oweh, H_owih, H_owoh, H_owuh
H_uwah, H_uweh, H_uwih, H_uwoh, H_uwuh

Seems overwhelming doesn't it? Yet, of these 50 possibilities only two provide Hebrew meanings. They are "havah" and "hovah." At first "hovah" appears to be the answer as in YA**HOVAH** (or with the "J" Ja**hovah** as in Je**hovah**), but the apparent meaning of "hovah" is: "to ruin, disaster" (Strong's #1943), therefore "hovah" does not seem to be the proper suffix for the Creator's name. The second choice, "havah" means: "to be, to become, to exist" (Strong's #1933b). Thus YA**HAVAH** is much more in line with the focus of the Creator's name. Especially when you consider that when He was asked what His name was by Moses, the Creator answered, "I AM THAT I AM" (Exodus 3:14).

However, there is the possibility that an ancient practice of abbreviation that revolves around the contraction of names[2] will provide more clues regarding the pronunciation of the Name. Rather than considering YAH to be drawn from the first two letters of Elohim's name (**YH**VH) we must consider that YAH is actually a contracted form of YHVH that is formed by a combination of the first and the last letters of **Y**HV**H** along with the vowel "a."

The possibility that YAH is a contraction rather than the first syllable of YHVH's name is supported by the fact that many Hebrew names use the syllable YAH as a suffix rather than as a prefix as seen in the following chart:

English	Hebrew	Transliteration	Meaning
Isaiah	ישעיהו	Yesha**yah**u	YHVH is Salvation
Elijah	אליהו	Eli**yah**u	YHVH is Elohim
Jeremiah	ירמיהו	Yirmi**yah**u	YHVH Exists

If the YAH in Psalms 68:4 and in halleluYAH is a contraction of YHVH's name rather than the first syllable of His name then just what is the first syllable? There are four possibilities: Y<u>e</u>H, Y<u>i</u>H, Y<u>o</u>H, and Y<u>u</u>H. Of these the most likely candidate is YeH. In the same way as YaH is used as a suffix in Hebrew naming, YeH is often used as a prefix. This type of naming is called "Theophoric" naming. Some Biblical examples of this type of naming are shown in the following chart:

English	Hebrew	Transliteration	Meaning
Jehoshaphat	יהושפט	**Yeh**oshafat	YHVH has judged
Jonathan	יהונתן	**Yeh**ohanan	YHVH has given
Joshua	יהושע	**Yeh**oshua	YHVH saves

Both of these charts seem to favor the use of YEH rather than YAH as the first syllable of Elohim's name—this means that rather than the name YAHavah we would pronounce Elohim's name as YEHavah. But what about YEHOVAH? YEHAVAH is so close to the generally accepted name JEHOVAH (Yehovah in Hebrew) that we know we must delve deeper and examine another clue regarding the Name.

If we examine "hovah" again we see that it was initially rejected because it appears to mean "ruin and disaster" whereas "havah" means "to be." However, upon further examination we find that hovah's root word in Hebrew is "havah" or "hayah" as in "to be, or to happen." Therefore "YeHOVAH" does have a meaning that makes sense for the Creator's name. Yet perhaps the strongest evidence in favor of "hovah" (as in YE-ho-vah) is that in Hebrew "YE" is the future tense of "to be" as in "*shall*", "HO" is the present tense of "to be" as in "*is*", and "AH" is the past tense of "to be" as in "*was*." The three parts of YE - HO - AH are seen in the three Hebrew verbs Yih**ye**h, **Ho**veh, and Hay**ah** meaning 'shall be,' 'is,' and 'was.'

Hebrew	Yih**ye**h	**Ho**veh	Hay**ah**
Meaning	*who* **shall be**	*who* **is**	*who* **was**
Syllable	**YE**	**HO**	**AH**

Thus YE-HO-AH can mean *"who shall be, who is, and who was.*[3]*"* This is in perfect alignment with YHVH's own words, "I am that I am." When we insert the VAV (V sound) we have the pronunciation of:

YE-HO-VAH

While we can't be absolutely sure that Elohim's name is pronounced as YEHOVAH, one thing is certain—the Name does have a pronunciation. Consider that even Moses wanted to know the name of the voice that spoke to him from the burning bush. Moses knew that if he followed the instruction of the voice—to go to the people of Israel in bondage in Egypt with the message given him—that the people would not believe him. Therefore he asked the voice to tell him who it was that was speaking. In one of the most famous verses in the Bible, the Father states:

> And Elohim said unto Moses, I AM THAT I AM: and he said, Thus shalt thou say unto the children of Israel, I AM hath sent me unto you.
>
> EXODUS 3:14

Most people think that the statement of the voice ends there. Even most preachers and evangelists stop there as well. But in the very next verse, which we have looked at earlier, the voice of our Elohim states His name clearly (remember that verse numbers were added to the text, therefore the next statement you are about to read is part of the original response of the Father to Moses—bold emphasis added):

> And Elohim said moreover unto Moses, Thus shalt thou say unto the children of Israel, **YEHOVAH** Elohim of your fathers, the Elohim of Abraham, the Elohim of Isaac, and the Elohim of Jacob, hath sent me unto you: **this *is* my name for ever**, and this *is* my memorial unto all generations.
>
> EXODUS 3:15

Based on what is written it is most likely that Moses told the people of Israel, "I AM THAT I AM sent me. His name forever is YEHOVAH. His name YEHOVAH is His memorial to all generations." And what is a memorial? Webster's defines memorial as: "*serving to preserve remembrance.*"

How shall we remember the name of Elohim if we are not told it, and how will we be told it if those who know it do not teach it, and how will our children know it unless we teach it to them? How will our family, our neighbors, our country and the world give honor and respect to the true Elohim, the Elohim of Abraham, Isaac, and Jacob, and the Father of Messiah Yehoshua (Jesus) unless we break the traditions of men that make the name of YEHOVAH of none-effect and

PROCLAIM HIS HOLY NAME!

The common people of ancient Israel knew and proclaimed Elohim's name. There are hundreds of Bible verses that prove that the Name was used and not hidden. One example of this is found the book of Ruth where we see Boaz (King David's great-grandfather) greet field workers with the name of YEHOVAH which he could not have done if he didn't know how to pronounce it:

> And, behold, Boaz came from Bethlehem, and said unto the reapers, YEHOVAH *be* with you. And they answered him, YEHOVAH bless thee.
>
> RUTH 2:4

Another powerful example is found in the book of Numbers chapter 6:22-27 where YEHOVAH instructs Moses in the manner that Aaron and his sons (Israel's Priests) should bless the children of Israel by saying (SPEAKING) His NAME over or upon them (bold emphasis added):

> And YEHOVAH spake unto Moses, saying, Speak unto Aaron and unto his sons, saying, On this wise ye shall bless the children of Israel, **saying** unto them,
>
> **YEHOVAH** bless thee, and keep thee:
>
> **YEHOVAH** make his face shine upon thee, and be gracious unto thee:
>
> **YEHOVAH** lift up his countenance upon thee, and give thee peace.
>
> And they shall **put my name** upon the children of Israel; and I will bless them.
>
> NUMBERS 6:22-27

Our heavenly Father makes it clear in Numbers 6:23 that the priests must SAY (speak out loud) His NAME over the children of Israel in order for them to be blessed by Him. He gave Moses the **exact** wording for this precious blessing and promise, and in Numbers 6:27 YEHOVAH makes it clear that by speaking this prayer His name is placed (put) upon the people.

It is then, **when His name is put upon the people**, that YEHOVAH will bless them!

YEHOVAH Proclaimed His Own Name

If someone wants you to know their name they simply tell you. YEHOVAH did just that—He spoke His own name to Moses and the Children of Israel over 70 times explicitly in the Torah. He did not hide it or tell Moses or the people that is was too holy to speak it.

The following table shows 25 of the over 70 verses where the Father proclaims His name (the complete list is found in Appendix A). We suggest that you take your time to read and consider each of the verses. Imagine you are there as YEHOVAH spoke. Feel the strength and love of the Father as he declares His own name:

Ex 6:2-3	And Elohim spake unto Moses, and said unto him, **I am YEHOVAH:** And I appeared unto Abraham, unto Isaac, and unto Jacob, by *the name of* El Shaddai but by **my name YEHOVAH** was I not known to them.
Ex 6:6	Wherefore say unto the children of Israel, **I am YEHOVAH**, and I will bring you out from under the burdens of the Egyptians, and I will rid you out of their bondage, and I will redeem you with a stretched out arm, and with great judgments:
Ex 6:7	And I will take you to me for a people, and I will be to you an Elohim: and ye shall know that **I am YEHOVAH** your Elohim, which bringeth you out from under the burdens of the Egyptians.

Ex 6:8	And I will bring you in unto the land, concerning the which I did swear to give it to Abraham, to Isaac, and to Jacob; and I will give it you for an heritage: **I am YEHOVAH**.
Ex 7:5	And the Egyptians shall know that **I am YEHOVAH**, when I stretch forth mine hand upon Egypt, and bring out the children of Israel from among them.
Ex 10:2	And that thou mayest tell in the ears of thy son, and of thy son's son, what things I have wrought in Egypt, and my signs which I have done among them; that ye may know how that **I am YEHOVAH**.
Ex 12:12	For I will pass through the land of Egypt this night, and will smite all the firstborn in the land of Egypt, both man and beast; and against all the elohim of Egypt I will execute judgment: **I am YEHOVAH.**
Ex 14:18	And the Egyptians shall know that **I am YEHOVAH**, when I have gotten me honour upon Pharaoh, upon his chariots, and upon his horsemen.
Ex 20:2-3	**I am YEHOVAH** thy Elohim, which have brought thee out of the land of Egypt, out of the house of bondage. Thou shalt have no other elohim before me.
Ex 29:46	And they shall know that **I am YEHOVAH** their Elohim, that brought them forth out of the land of Egypt, that I may dwell among them: **I am YEHOVAH** their Elohim.
Ex 31:13	Speak thou also unto the children of Israel, saying, Verily my sabbaths ye shall keep: for it *is* a sign between me and you throughout your generations; that *ye* may know that **I am YEHOVAH** that doth sanctify you.

Lev 11:45	For **I *am* YEHOVAH** that bringeth you up out of the land of Egypt, to be your Elohim: ye shall therefore be holy, for I *am* holy.
Lev 18:2	Speak unto the children of Israel, and say unto them, **I am YEHOVAH** your Elohim.
Lev 18:5	Ye shall therefore keep my statutes, and my judgments: which if a man do, he shall live in them: **I *am* YEHOVAH**.
Lev 19:3	Ye shall fear every man his mother, and his father, and keep my sabbaths: **I *am* YEHOVAH** your Elohim.
Lev 19:28	Ye shall not make any cuttings in your flesh for the dead, nor print any marks upon you: **I *am* YEHOVAH**.
Lev 19:30	Ye shall keep my sabbaths, and reverence my sanctuary: **I *am* YEHOVAH**.
Lev 19:31	Regard not them that have familiar spirits, neither seek after wizards, to be defiled by them: **I *am* YEHOVAH** your Elohim.
Lev 19:34	*But* the stranger that dwelleth with you shall be unto you as one born among you, and thou shalt love him as thyself; for ye were strangers in the land of Egypt: **I *am* YEHOVAH** your Elohim.
Lev 22:31	Therefore shall ye keep my commandments, and do them: **I *am* YEHOVAH**.
Lev 22:32	Neither shall ye profane my holy name; but I will be hallowed among the children of Israel: **I *am* YEHOVAH** which hallow you,
Lev 24:22	Ye shall have one manner of law, as well for the stranger, as for one of your own country: for **I *am* YEHOVAH** your Elohim.

Lev 25:17	Ye shall not therefore oppress one another; but thou shalt fear thy Elohim: for **I *am* YEHOVAH** your Elohim.
Lev 26:2	Ye shall keep my sabbaths, and reverence my sanctuary: **I *am* YEHOVAH**.
Num 15:41	**I *am* YEHOVAH** your Elohim, which brought you out of the land of Egypt, to be your Elohim: **I *am* YEHOVAH** your Elohim.

Has the Name Really Been Lost?

The fact that the pronunciation of the Name has apparently been lost over the centuries or worse—hidden from the world—is a sad testament of the priestly class of Judaism. The nation that agreed to be a nation of priests unto YEHOVAH has failed to follow YEHOVAH's desire for His name to be known, honored, *and* used:

> And it shall come to pass, *that* whosoever shall call on the name of YEHOVAH shall be **delivered**: for in mount Zion and in Jerusalem shall be deliverance, as YEHOVAH hath said, and in the remnant whom the YEHOVAH shall call.
>
> JOEL 2:32

How can we call on His name if we don't know it or how to pronounce it? How will the people be delivered? Fortunately, there is a concerted effort by many sincere people, including Jews such as Nehemia Gordon, who are working to uncover and proclaim the Father's name. Rather than follow Rabbinic oral prohibitions or Christian traditions regarding the Name they have undertaken a serious inquiry to uncover the Father's name and proclaim it to the world. Let us all join in and speak the Name to the best of our abilities as we reach out to our Creator, our Father, YEHOVAH.

> Then they that feared YEHOVAH spake often one to another: and YEHOVAH hearkened, and heard *it*, and a book of remembrance was written before him for them that feared YEHOVAH, and that thought upon his name.
>
> MALACHI 3:16

Chapter 4

Who is the Messiah and What is His Name?

> Who hath ascended up into heaven, or descended? Who hath gathered the wind in his fists? Who hath bound the waters in a garment? Who hath established all the ends of the earth? What *is* his name, and what *is* his son's name, if thou canst tell?
>
> PROVERBS 30:4

The Messiah is a figure central to Jewish culture as the anticipated saviour of the Jews. The Hebrew word for Messiah is *Mashiach* which means "*anointed.*" There are no references to the word "messiah" in the King James New Testament (however the word "messias" is used twice). Rather than use a word that more closely resembled the actual Hebrew word *Mashiach*, the King James translators used an English form of the Greek word *Christos* in their translations. Hence we read about Jesus *Christ* rather than Messiah Jesus. This has hindered most Christians' understanding of the Hebrew roots of their faith.

Even though Jewish tradition speaks of two Messiahs: Messiah Ben Joseph (the Messiah as the suffering servant) and Messiah Ben David (the Messiah as the ruling King) most Jews do not accept that the Messiah has already come. They do not accept Jesus as the suffering servant who was sacrificed as the atonement for sin and who defeated death and Satan.

While the Jews do believe that a Messiah will someday arise, they do not believe that the Messiah will be the Son of YEHOVAH. They believe it is blasphemy to say that YEHOVAH has a son (Mark 14:61-64). Yet the Tanakh (Hebrew Bible) clearly shows that YEHOVAH has a son as written in Proverbs 30:4 above. Additionally, Moses wrote of a special prophet that YEHOVAH would raise up, a prophet of Israel of the stature of Moses, who would speak all the words that YEHOVAH would give him. Christians believe that this prophet is Jesus—the Son of YEHOVAH:

> I will raise them up a Prophet from among their brethren, like unto thee, and will put my words in his mouth; and he shall speak unto them all that I shall command him.
>
> DEUTERONOMY 18:18

Who is the Messiah and What is His Name?

It is interesting that the word *raise* is used in the verse above—for three reasons. First, a father "*raises up a son,*" so it could be inferred that the prophet is to be the son of the Father—reinforcing the fact that YEHOVAH has a son. Second, the Messiah would be *raised* (lifted up) on the cross as a sacrifice for our sin thereby providing us a way to eternal life (John 3:14-16). Third, that the Messiah was *raised* up after his crucifixion—defeating death and Satan—by his Father's power (Galatians 1:1).

The Jews knew of and were awaiting the special prophet written of in Deuteronomy 18:18. When John the Baptist was being questioned by the representatives of the Pharisees (who were sent to find out who John was) they asked him specifically if he was *the* prophet:

> And they asked him, What then? Art thou Elias? And he saith, I am not. Art thou that prophet? And he answered, No.
>
> JOHN 1:21

The Jews also knew that YEHOVAH had proclaimed a curse regarding the prophet. As you will see in the chapter on blessings and curses, the Jews were very concerned about making a mistake regarding the prophet to come:

> And it shall come to pass, *that* whosoever will not hearken unto my words which he [the prophet] shall speak in my name, I will require *it* of him.
>
> DEUTERONOMY 18:19

To the modern reader the phrase "I will require it of him" is somewhat obscure. It means that whoever does not listen to the prophet to come, the one who is to be of the stature of Moses, will bear the judgment of YEHOVAH.

While the vast majority of Jews do not believe that the Messiah has appeared, there are 2.1 billion people or roughly 30% of the Earth's living population that believe he has. Yet most of these people, while they have the correct historic personality, use a name that simply cannot be his given name: Jesus. As shown in a prior chapter, the letter "J" didn't exist in English until the 1500's and the letter "J" has never existed in Hebrew. It is extremely unlikely that the Messiah was ever called Jesus when he was on Earth.

Just as Rabbinic tradition obscured the name of the Creator, it is the Christian Church itself that has obscured the Messiah's name. Rather than seeking out and proclaiming the true Hebrew name of the Messiah they have instead translated a hybrid name from

Greek manuscripts that changes the Messiah's name into a word unrecognizable by the Jewish nation he was born into. We've inherited an incorrect translation of the Messiah's name without question—because we have trusted in men and their traditions.

The New Testament Greek word translated as Jesus is ιησου (pronounced as *Iēsous* or some say *Yesoos*). If one believes only in the Word as it was originally written in Greek then they would need to speak the name *Iēsous* when referring to the Messiah as that is the pronunciation of the word from the original manuscripts certainly not 'Jesus' with the 'gee' sound in English. In fact, *Iēsous* (as Iesus) was used as the name of the Messiah in the original edition of the King James Bible in 1611 as well as other Christian Bibles as late as the 17th Century. Was *Iēsous* really the name and sound that was delivered to Joseph?

> But while he thought on these things, behold, the angel of YEHOVAH appeared unto him in a dream, saying, Joseph, thou son of David, fear not to take unto thee Mary thy wife: for that which is conceived in her is of the Holy Ghost. And she shall bring forth a son, and thou shalt call his name JESUS: for he shall save his people from their sins.
> MATTHEW 1:20-21

Did the angel of YEHOVAH speak to Joseph a name that has a sound never uttered in Hebrew—Jesus? Did he speak to Joseph in Greek—Iēsous? Did the name Jesus even have a Hebrew meaning at the time of the dream? We believe the answer to all three questions is absolutely *not*.

While the angel could have given Joseph a nonsensical name for his son and then explained that the name meant *"He shall save his people from their sins,"* there is another Hebrew name that closely matches that specific meaning. It is Yehoshua (or in English Joshua). The meaning of Yehoshua in Hebrew is "YEHOVAH is salvation" or "YEHOVAH saves." Yehoshua is also the name of Moses's second in command, the man who was considered a hero by the children of Israel, who led them to victory in their battles and who led them into the promised land.

Joseph, a devout Jew, would have been aware of the scriptures regarding the naming of people by YEHOVAH. He would have understood the importance of choosing the proper name for his child. He would have certainly been familiar and comfortable with the name Yehoshua as opposed to Jesus, or more accurately *Iēsous*, both of which would have sounded odd and alien to him and meant nothing in the Hebrew language.

Clues in the Septuagint and the Greek New Testament

Perhaps one of the most significant clues that prove that the Messiah's name should not be translated as Jesus is also found in the name of Joshua and how it was translated in the English Old Testament from the Greek Septuagint and in the English New Testament from the Greek New Testament.

First we will examine the Septuagint—which is the accepted scholarly Greek version of the original Hebrew Bible (translated in the 3rd century B.C. *before* there was a New Testament). In it we find that the Hebrew name Yehoshua (Joshua) is translated exclusively over 450 times (except for three instances) as *Iēsous*. Therefore Joshua and *Iēsous* are synonymous. In other words the name *Joshua* = *Iēsous* = *Yehoshua*.

The following is an example from the original Hebrew text, the Septuagint translation from Hebrew to Greek, and the King James English translation from Greek to English (transliterated for ease of pronunciation):

<u>In Original Hebrew text:</u>
Vay•tzav **Yeho•shoo•a** et-shot•rei ha•am le•mor,

JOSHUA 1:10

<u>In the Septuagint (Hebrew to Greek):</u>
kai eneteilato **Iēsous** tois grammateusin tou laou legōn

JOSHUA 1:10

<u>In English (Greek to English):</u>
Then **Joshua** commanded the officers of the people, saying,

JOSHUA 1:10

The three times in the Septuagint the name Yehoshua was not translated as *Iēsous* are found in Numbers 13:16 and I Chronicles 7:27 where it is translated as *Iēsoun* and *Iēsoue* respectively as well as in Nehemiah 8:17 where it is translated as *Iēsou* (from the Hebrew Yeshua—the short form of Yehoshua):

<u>In Hebrew (transliterated):</u>
...ki lo-asoo miy•mei **Ye•shoo•a** Bin-Noon ken b'nei Israel ad ha•yom...

NEHEMIAH 8:17

<u>In Greek (transliterated from the Septuagint):</u>
...en skēnais oti ouk epoiēsan apo ēmerōn **Iēsou** uiou nauē outōs oi uioi israēl...

NEHEMIAH 8:17

Who is the Messiah and What is His Name?

<u>In English:</u>
> ...for since the days of **Jeshua** the son of Nun unto that day had not the children of Israel done so...
> NEHEMIAH 8:17

Joshua also appears in the original Greek *New Testament* as the Greek word *Iēsous*. His name only appears twice (Acts 7:45 and Hebrews 4:8). Upon close examination of these two verses you will find that the King James version of the Bible oddly translates the Greek word *Iēsous* into English as Jesus rather than Joshua, which clearly does not fit the context. Virtually all other translations use the name Joshua (the son of Nun). First we will review Acts 7:45:

> which also our fathers having in succession received, did bring in with **Joshua**, into the possession of the nations whom Elohim did drive out from the presence of our fathers, till the days of David,
> ACTS 7:45 (YLT)

> Which also our fathers that came after brought in with **Jesus** into the possession of the Gentiles, whom Elohim drave out be-

fore the face of our fathers, unto the days of David;

ACTS 7:45 (KJV)

Next we will review the reference to Joshua in Hebrews 4:8:

since then, it remaineth for certain to enter into it, and those who did first hear good news [the children of Israel] entered not in [to the promised land] because of unbelief -- again He [Elohim] doth limit a certain day, 'To-day,' (in David saying, after so long a time,) as it hath been said, 'To-day, if His voice ye may hear, ye may not harden your hearts,' for if **Joshua** had given them rest, He would not concerning another day have spoken after these things;

HEBREWS 4:6-8 (YLT)

Seeing therefore it remaineth that some must enter therein, and they to whom it was first preached entered not in because of unbelief: Again, he limiteth a certain day, saying in David, To day, after so long a time; as it is said, To day if ye will hear his voice, harden not your hearts. For if **Jesus**

had given them rest, then would he not afterward have spoken of another day.
HEBREWS 4:6-8 (KJV)

Acts 7:45 is clearly speaking of the original covenant patriarchs and not the Messiah and in Hebrews 4:8 Paul is referring to the children of Israel who didn't enter into the promised land because of their unbelief. So why did the King James translators use the name Jesus instead of Joshua in these two passages? Either the translators of the King James didn't have enough discernment to see that the references were to the original covenant Joshua; or they wanted to mask the fact that the name of the Messiah came from a Hebrew root word; or they wanted the Messiah's name to be unique. Unfortunately for them, men don't get to choose the name of the Messiah—his name came to us from the Creator.

Untangling the Messiah's name

You can't have it both ways. One Greek name (*Iēsous*) cannot be translated as two different English names (Joshua and Jesus). The following chart shows how the Hebrew Yehoshua was translated into Greek and then shows that the Greek name was split into two different English names:

Language	Joshua into Jesus	
Hebrew (original text)	Yehoshua	
Greek (Septuagint and Greek New Testament)	Iēsous	
Old English (1611 King James Old and New Testaments)	Ioshua	Iesus
English (Modern English Bibles)	Joshua	Jesus

It is clear from the Septuagint, which was written hundreds of years before the New Testament, and the two references in the New Testament (Acts 7:45 and Hebrews 4:8) that *Iēsous* was translated from the Hebrew name "Yehoshua" and then into the English as Joshua. To translate the vast majority of the occurrences of the word *Iēsous* later as Jesus instead of Joshua throughout the whole New Testament is an unfortunate fabrication that has caused the true name of the Messiah to be hidden from the vast majority of both Christians and non-Christians alike. But by the grace of Elohim the Hebraic roots movement is rapidly changing this blindness and more and more people are coming to learn the Messiah's true name.

Another clue that the Messiah's original given name is Yehoshua is how some Jewish writings referred to Yehoshua after his death: Yeshu. The meaning of Yeshu is hidden in the acronym YSHU or "**Y**emach **Sh**mo **u**'Zikro" transliterated. In Hebrew this phrase means: "may his name be blotted out." By leaving off the "a" from "Yeshua" (the short form of Yehoshua) every time someone spoke the Messiah's name as "Yeshu" they were, in essence, cursing him—with one of the strongest curses that a Jewish person could utter.

Does the Messiah really care what name he is called by? Consider first that *all* that the Son did was what he saw the Father do (John 5:19). We have shown in the first chapters of this book and will continue to show in subsequent chapters that YEHOVAH cares deeply that His true name be proclaimed to all ends of the Earth. The Messiah therefore also wishes for his true name to be proclaimed as well.

> And whatsoever ye shall ask in **my name**, that will I do, that the Father may be glorified in the Son.
>
> JOHN 14:13

Next, consider Matthew 12:21. This short verse contains a deep prophetic promise that relies totally on knowing the true name of the Messiah. How does one trust in the name if one does not know the true name?

> And in his name shall the Gentiles trust.
> MATTHEW 12:21

It is also important to note that the first part of the Creator's name is embedded in Yehoshua's name:

◄────── Read right to left

Yehovah	יְהוָה
Yehoshua	יְהוֹשֻׁעַ

It is in this name, Yehoshua, that the disciples both taught and healed in after the Holy Ghost had come upon them. It is also the name that the religious leaders forbade the disciples to speak on behalf of:

> ...and when they had called the apostles, and beaten *them*, they commanded that they should not speak in the name of Yehoshua, and let them go.
> ACTS 5:40

Who is the Messiah and What is His Name?

The Messiah prophesied this persecution of his followers:

> Remember the word that I said unto you, The servant is not greater than his master. If they have persecuted me, they will also persecute you; if they have kept my saying, they will keep yours also. But all these things will they do unto you for **my name's sake**, because they know not him that sent me.
>
> JOHN 15:20-21

Once again, just as with the Creator's name, there is not complete agreement on the Hebrew name of the Messiah. However, the commonly accepted Hebrew names of the Messiah are: Yehoshua, Yeshua, Y'shua, and Yahshua.

We are personally comfortable addressing the Messiah with either: Yehoshua, Yeshua, Y'shua, or Yahshua. Any one of these names gets us exponentially closer to the Messiah's Elohim-given name than does the Greek *Iēsous* or the English *Jesus*. However, we are more inclined towards the name "Yehoshua" which means "Yehovah saves." The first part **YEHO** refers to YEHOVAH—as in **Yeho**vah and the last syllable **SHUA** means "*saves.*"

Both Yehoshua, the son of Nun, and Messiah Yehoshua, the son of *none* (no *Earthly* father) fulfilled the meaning and purpose of their names: *"Yehovah saves."* Yehoshua's (son of Nun) mission was to bring the children of Israel into the promised land while Messiah Yehoshua's mission was to bring fallen mankind into the promise of eternal life as "Sons of Elohim" (John 1:12).

So does it really matter which name we use to refer to the Messiah? How would you feel if someone chose to call you by another name, a name you were not known by, which gave credit to your achievements and sacrifices to another? For example, when we (Linda and Peter) were married our surname changed. We put both of our last names together to form a new name: Miller-Russo. But even to this day some family and friends refuse to address us by our new name. We don't hold this against them, but we find it odd that they cling to the past and do not honor the present.

Likewise, many Christian preachers continue to use "Jesus" rather than the Messiah's real name most likely because it is easier for them to go along with tradition rather than change. They may also resist teaching their congregation the true name of the Messiah for fear of upsetting their flock and potentially losing their financial support.

Who is the Messiah and What is His Name?

> For they loved the praise of men more than
> the praise of Elohim.
>
> JOHN 12:43

As Yehoshua's sacrifice was placed before us to choose to believe or not believe; to accept the blood redemption or to reject it; so too have you been given the choice to challenge your traditions and use the Messiah's Hebrew name—Yehoshua—the name which was given to him by YEHOVAH and which has been placed before you today.

In this chapter we have replaced the title "the LORD" with YEHOVAH and will do so for the remainder of this book. Also for the remainder of this book the name Jesus will be replaced with the Hebrew *Yehoshua*. New Testament references to "the Lord" or "Lord" (lower case) have been changed to YEHOVAH, master, or saviour depending upon the context of the verse. For example, in Luke 4:18-19 where Yehoshua is reading from the scroll of Isaiah (61:1-2) some Bibles translate the name YHVH from Hebrew to lower case "the Lord" or upper case "G_D" even though the verses are explicitly referring to YEHOVAH's name. For another example of this compare Jeremiah 31:31-34 with Hebrews 8:8-12.

Other Biblical names have been left alone however for ease of reading. The purpose of changing "the LORD" to YEHOVAH and Jesus to Yehoshua is to highlight the actual names of the Father and His Son (Messiah), to do them honor and to break the "traditions-of-men" spirit that has covered the Jewish and Christian churches for far too long.

Chapter 5

THE FULFILLMENT OF THE LAW

I *am* YEHOVAH thy Elohim, which have brought thee out of the land of Egypt, out of the house of bondage. Thou shalt have no other elohim before me. Thou shalt not make unto thee any graven image, or any likeness *of any thing* that *is* in heaven above, or that *is* in the earth beneath, or that *is* in the water under the earth: Thou shalt not bow down thyself to them, nor serve them: for I YEHOVAH thy Elohim *am* a jealous [zealous] Elohim, visiting the iniquity of the fathers upon the children unto the third and fourth *generation* of them that hate me; And shewing mercy unto thousands of them that love me, and keep my commandments.

Exodus 20: 2-6

In the verses above (which detail the first of the Ten Commandments) the Creator makes it very clear that

He desires us to know, glorify, and honor Him alone. He is our Mighty One, our all. He alone is to be looked to, above all others, to guide us in right living, for by His standards righteousness can be discerned. In the verses above the Creator even equates loving Him with *obeying* His commands: "them that love me, **and** keep my commandments." Very few of us who believe in Him will have a problem with the first commandment; however His instructions for our welfare go deeper. In Exodus 23:13 the Creator commands:

> And in all *things* that I have said unto you be circumspect: and make no mention of the name of other elohim, neither let it be heard out of thy mouth.
> EXODUS 23:13

In addition to the command to not utter the names of other mighty ones, YEHOVAH went a step further and actually required the children of Israel to *destroy* the names of other elohim so that they would be remembered no more:

> And ye shall overthrow their altars, and break their pillars, and burn their groves with fire; and ye shall hew down the graven images of their elohim, and **destroy** the

names of them out of that place.
>
> DEUTERONOMY 12:3

"Destroy" is translated from the Hebrew word *"ve·'ib·bad·tem"*—which actually means to *"obliterate."* Destroy and obliterate are somewhat different. "Destroy" has a more materialistic bent, i.e., to bust apart, as in the pagan altars and pillars. Even though the word "obliterate" could be used in the same materialistic way, it leans more towards a *"total removal"* of the offending object. Webster online defines "obliterate" as: *"to remove utterly from recognition or memory."* Therefore, another way to translate the verse with this in mind is:

> And ye shall overthrow their altars, and break their pillars, and burn their groves with fire; and ye shall hew down the graven images of their elohim, and **obliterate** the names of them out of that place.
>
> DEUTERONOMY 12:3

And then to emphasize the importance of the Creator's name YEHOVAH immediately states that we should not do the same to Him and His name. In other words we should NOT remove His name from recognition or memory:

> Ye shall not do so unto YEHOVAH your Elohim.
>
> DEUTERONOMY 12:4

The prophet Isaiah makes a reference to this command of YEHOVAH in Isaiah 26:13:

> O YEHOVAH our Elohim, *other* elohim beside thee have had dominion over us: *but* by thee only will we make mention of thy name.
>
> ISAIAH 26:13

We agree with Isaiah, so we too will honor the Father by not mentioning the names of other elohim throughout the pages of this book. However, there is at least one word commonly used in Western culture to refer to the Creator that causes people to inadvertently break YEHOVAH's command in Exodus 23:13. While the following may be difficult for some to consider (let alone accept) it needs to be stated. The word that causes people to inadvertently break YEHOVAH's command is the standard English word for the Supreme Being: "G_d." And no, we didn't spell it as "G_d" to acknowledge Rabbinic tradition, we spelled it as "G_d" because, in essence, the sound of the word is the same sound as the name of another pagan de-

The Fulfillment of the Law

ity—a name we should not utter or mention: "Ga_." While you may think it strange that we don't spell the complete word, we will not do so in order to follow the command of the Creator (note: while we will remove a letter from the name of other elohim within the remainder of the text of this book any Bible verses that contain the name(s) of other elohim will not be altered).

In the original Hebrew text of Isaiah 65:11 a reference is made to a Syrio-Babylonian deity. The deity's name "Ga_" is translated as "fortune" or "good fortune" in most English Bibles. The worship of "Ga_" is from ancient Syrian origins where it is believed the people mixed worship of the false deity with YEHOVAH.[1]

The name "Ga_" was given by Leah, Jacob's wife, to a son born by her handmaiden Zilpah. The fact that Leah picked the name of a false deity however is not commonly know. Leah was taught the ways of the Syrians by her father Laban.[2] She actually named her son "Ga_" because of her *good fortune*.

> Then Leah said, "How fortunate!" So she named him Gad.
> GENESIS 30:11 (NAS)

Leah's good fortune was likely her belief that the more sons she could give Jacob, the more he would choose to love her over her sister Rachel who was also

Jacob's wife.

While a direct link between "Ga_" and "G_d" cannot be made the spoken sound of the original Hebrew "Ga_" (*gawd*) is the same as the English pronunciation of the word "G_d." Even if coincidental, millions unwittingly address YEHOVAH with the sound of the name of a pagan deity. While it is certainly unintentional it is still true nevertheless that when people worship, preach, and converse using the term "G_d" the sound coming out of their mouths is the sound of the pagan deity's name.

In addition to the sound of the word "G_d" being identical to the sound of a pagan deity, the word itself is from suspect origins. In middle age Germanic cultures the word "G_d" was a short form of a pagan deity "G_dan" (which is derived from the Norse mythological deity called "Od_n").[3]

In an interesting side note consider that the phrase "Egads" (which some sources claim was used by the ancient Romans and Greeks while others believe it is from the 17th century) means "Oh G_d."[4]

Considering the mix-up of languages at the tower of Babel and mankind's historic worship of pagan deities it seems reasonable that the various words to describe the pagan deities have cross-migrated between cultures over the centuries.

Some may say that we are not under the law and therefore it doesn't matter what word one uses to address YEHOVAH. However, by speaking the names of other mighty ones from their lips they are disregarding the Creator's command in Exodus 23:13. While we acknowledge that the Messiah is our redemption, the payment for our sin, the Messiah himself warned us:

> Not every one that saith unto me, Master, Master, shall enter into the kingdom of heaven; but he that doeth the **will of my Father** which is in heaven.
> MATTHEW 7:21

Is lawlessness—the disobeying of the Father's will—part of Messiah's teaching? Absolutely not. He did not come to destroy the law but to fulfill the law. In Matthew 5:17 the Messiah states:

> Think not that I am come to destroy the law, or the prophets: I am not come to destroy, but to fulfill.
> MATTHEW 5:17

And what is the fulfillment of the law? The Greek word translated in this verse to "fulfill" is *plērōsai*. It means *"to fill"* or *"to complete."* It doesn't mean to abolish or overthrow the law. However, the Greek word *kataluo* translated to *"destroy"* in the verse above does mean *"to abolish or overthrow."* Misinterpretations of this verse by those who claim that the Messiah's fulfillment of the law actually abolished the law are in a sense translating the verse as:

> Think not that I am come to destroy the law, or the prophets: I am not come to **destroy** the law, but to **destroy** it.
> MATTHEW 5:17

Does that make sense?

The fulfillment of the law—its completion in the Messiah—is what the prophet Jeremiah prophesied:

> Behold, the days come, saith YEHOVAH, that I will make a new covenant with the house of Israel, and with the house of Judah: Not according to the covenant that I made with their fathers in the day *that* I took them by the hand to bring them out of the land of Egypt; which my covenant they brake, although I was an husband unto them, saith YEHOVAH: But this *shall be* the covenant that I will make with the house of

> Israel; After those days, saith YEHOVAH, I will put my law in their inward parts, and write it in their hearts; and will be their Elohim, and they shall be my people.
>
> JEREMIAH 31:31-33

This new covenant, sealed with Messiah's blood, binds us even closer to the law of YEHOVAH for the Messiah said: *"If ye love me, do my commandments"* and Yehoshua's commandments are the will of the Father:

> For I have not spoken of myself [Yehoshua]; but the Father [YEHOVAH] which sent me, he gave me a commandment, what I should say, and what I should speak. And I know that his commandment is life everlasting: whatsoever I speak therefore, even as the Father said unto me, so I speak.
>
> JOHN 12:49-50

The Messiah gave many commandments, all for our benefit, which as shown above came from the Father. His commandments can be summarized as "Love YEHOVAH your Elohim with all your heart, soul, and mind and love your neighbor as yourself." Let us honor the Messiah and show him our love for him by doing (following) his commandments:

> And Yehoshua said to him, 'Thou shalt love YEHOVAH thy Elohim with all thy heart, and with all thy soul, and with all thine understanding—this is a first and great command; and the second is like to it, Thou shalt love thy neighbor as thyself; on these—the two commands—all the law and the prophets do hang.'
>
> MATTHEW 22:37-40 (YLT)

Chapter 6

THE PROPHECY OF MALACHI

> A son honoureth *his* father, and a servant his master: if then I *be* a father, where *is* mine honour? and if I *be* a master, where *is* my fear? saith YEHOVAH of hosts unto you, O priests, that despise my name. And ye say, Wherein have we despised thy name?
>
> MALACHI 1:6

The book of Malachi was written between 440 and 400 B.C. Its author is assumed to be a prophet called Malachi. While the writing style is similar to some of the other known prophets of the Hebrew bible, there is no scholarly consensus as to the actual author.

The word Malachi in Hebrew means "*My Messenger.*" One would rightly assume that the "My" refers to YEHOVAH, the Elohim of Abraham, Isaac, and Jacob. According to some sources Malachi is a shortened form of the word "Malakhiyah" which would equate to

"Messenger of Yah" as in Malakhi-YAH. Fundamentally, this would provide additional validation that the author is YEHOVAH's messenger. As a message from YEHOVAH, the book of Malachi contains several key verses related to the Name, specifically Malachi 1:11 (below) and Malachi 4:2 (shown later) that hold special importance to those who love Elohim:

> For from the rising of the sun even unto the going down of the same my **name** *shall be* great among the Gentiles; and in every place incense *shall be* offered unto my **name**, and a pure offering: for my **name** *shall be* great among the heathen, saith YEHOVAH of hosts.
>
> MALACHI 1:11

In the verse above YEHOVAH proclaims that His name shall be great among the Gentiles and that incense will be offered to Him, as a pure offering. Therefore, those who are to be a part of this divine prophecy, the Gentiles (everyone that is not Israel) will offer incense unto YEHOVAH's name, not to the word "name" but to His name: YEHOVAH. And it must be a pure offering; in other words not done with ulterior motives.

Has YEHOVAH's name been made great to the Gentiles yet? Have the Western Churches fulfilled this proclamation of Yehoshua's father? Have they offered incense to His *name*? The answer to all three questions is no. To the contrary, the Gentile religious establishment has hidden His name, changing over 6800 references to it in the Bible to a mere title—"the LORD." The closest fulfillment of this prophecy that the authors, Linda and Peter, have experienced was when they attended high mass as children in the Catholic Church. The priest would swing an incense holder during a portion of the mass. However, there was not one audible reference to the Name nor whether the incense was meant as an offering to Elohim, let alone to the name YEHOVAH. Making something obscure does not make it great.

If you read the verses surrounding Malachi 1:11 you will find that the priestly class is being chastised by YEHOVAH. He accuses them of despising His name, of showing Him no honor and He goes on to explain the nature of these trespasses against Him:

* They offered lame, sick, and blind animals for sacrifice in the Temple instead of animals without physical defects.
* They offered polluted bread on YEHOVAH's altar defiled by their statements that YEHOVAH's altar has no value.

YEHOVAH goes on to say that He even longs for someone to shut the Temple doors so that these abominable sacrifices would cease. Stop and think for a moment; what type of offerings, sacrifices, and religious practices do we participate in today that may elicit a similar reaction from our Creator? Perhaps dyeing "Ea_ter" (name of a pagan deity) eggs to celebrate the Messiah's resurrection or decorating a tree with pagan symbols to celebrate the Messiah's birth? Pastors and believers need to conscientiously examine the Word for guidance regarding YEHOVAH's will about the pagan *traditions of men*. Remember that the Church has been grafted in; we are to be one with the chosen *set-apart* Hebrew nation. Therefore we are to be separate from the world, and this would include pagan "religious" celebrations not found in the Word.

To further describe the value that YEHOVAH places on His name, He gives an ominous warning (curse) to the priests:

> If ye will not hear, and if ye will not lay *it* to heart, to give glory unto my **name**, saith YEHOVAH of hosts, I will even send a curse upon you, and I will curse your blessings: yea, I have cursed them already, because ye do not lay *it* to heart.
>
> MALACHI 2:2

Glory to His name—that is what YEHOVAH desires—in your heart! Glory is defined as *"praise, honor, or distinction extended by common consent."* YEHOVAH desires it to the point of canceling out the blessings bestowed by Him on His chosen clerics. He still desires glory for His name today. YEHOVAH is unchanging and steadfast:

> For I *am* YEHOVAH, I change not; therefore ye sons of Jacob are not consumed.
> MALACHI 3:6

Yet even centuries after the book of Malachi was written it is very rare to hear pastors and evangelists proclaiming the name of YEHOVAH. They speak *about* the name, but don't actually *say* it or *teach* the actual name. How is the name of YEHOVAH honored if it's not spoken and no one knows what it is? In Malachi 2:7-9 the messenger writes:

> For the priest's lips should keep knowledge, and they should seek the law at his mouth: for he *is* the messenger of YEHOVAH of hosts. But ye are departed out of the way; ye have caused many to stumble at the law; ye have corrupted the covenant of Levi, saith YEHOVAH of hosts.

> Therefore have I also made you contempt-
> ible and base before all the people, accord-
> ing as ye have not kept my ways, but have
> been partial in the law.
>
> MALACHI 2:7-9

YEHOVAH commands that His name be honored and proclaimed to all people, yet the religious teachers and preachers of today, like the priests spoken about in the book of Malachi, still do not obey YEHOVAH's command. Somehow they believe that they can ignore His name while at the same time imploring Him to meet their needs. Most church organizations believe that they can follow only nine of the ten commandments, changing YEHOVAH's perpetual Sabbath day from Saturday to Sunday by their own authority (see Exodus 31:16-17 for YEHOVAH's instructions). Others omit the second commandment and take the tenth and split it into two in order to still have ten. By doing this they mislead their parishioners into believing that it is okay to have graven images in their churches—thus breaking the first commandment of Elohim as well. They love the *"traditions of men"* more than honoring the Word of YEHOVAH.

In direct contrast to the warnings (curses) given to the priests in Malachi 2:7-9, YEHOVAH promises that others will receive great blessings regarding His name.

> For, behold, the day cometh, that shall burn as an oven; and all the proud, yea, and all that do wickedly, shall be stubble: and the day that cometh shall burn them up, saith YEHOVAH of hosts, that it shall leave them neither root nor branch. But unto **you that fear my name** shall the Sun of righteousness arise with healing in his wings; and ye shall go forth, and grow up as calves of the stall. And ye shall tread down the wicked; for **they shall be ashes** under the soles of your feet in the day that I shall do *this*, saith YEHOVAH of hosts.
> MALACHI 4:1-3

The contrast is clear. The wicked, those that twist YEHOVAH's Word, and the proud ones that believe their works are greater than His shall be turned to ash—nothing left but ash. But those who fear the Name will have the "Sun of righteousness" minister to them, bringing healing.

"Fearing" the Name does not mean to be afraid, as in a "fear" of flying. "Fear" as used in this verse means *"to have a reverential awe of."* "Reverential" or "revered" means a *"profound adoring awed respect."*

So the verse could have been translated as:

> But unto you that have **profound adoring awed respect for my name** shall the Sun of righteousness arise with healing in his wings; and ye shall go forth, and grow up as calves of the stall.
>
> MALACHI 4:2

The reference to "in his wings" refers to the tassels on a Jewish prayer shawl's four corners which are meant to remind the wearer of the Torah (instructions) of YEHOVAH (Numbers 15:37-41). Even more important is that the *"Sun of righteousness shall arise with healing in his wings"* refers to Messiah Yehoshua's healing power. We know this through the miracle healings of the sick when they touched the "hem of his garment" (the tassels on the corners of Messiah's *tallit*—his prayer shawl). A case in point is the miracle healing of the woman with the issue of blood who thought, "If I may but touch his garment I shall be whole" (Matthew 9:20-22). In addition to this woman many others sought and received miracle healings through the fulfillment of the promise of YEHOVAH:

> And when they were gone over, they came into the land of Gennesaret. And when

> the men of that place had knowledge of him [Yehoshua], they sent out into all that country round about, and brought unto him **all** that were diseased; And besought him that they might only **touch the hem of his garment**: and as many as touched were made perfectly whole.
> MATTHEW 14:34-36

This wonderful healing promise from our Father in Malachi 4:2 is available even today for those who have a profound adoring awed respect (fear) for YEHOVAH's name. Let us give His name glory like His Son Yehoshua taught us in "the Lord's Prayer."

> After this manner therefore pray ye: Our Father which art in heaven, Hallowed be thy name. Thy kingdom come. Thy will be done in earth, as *it is* in heaven. Give us this day our daily bread. And forgive us our debts, as we forgive our debtors. And lead us not into temptation, but deliver us from evil: For thine is the kingdom, and the power, and the glory, for ever. Amen.
> MATTHEW 6:9-13

Proclaim His Holy Name

Chapter 7

BLESSINGS AND CURSES

> The curse of YEHOVAH *is* in the house of the wicked: but he blesseth the habitation of the just.
>
> PROVERBS 3:33

What is the difference between a wicked person and a just person? Consider two words from the verse above; the word "wicked" and the word "just." The root of the word wicked is "wick." Just as a candle's wick is twisted, a wicked person is twisted, i.e., they "see" the world in a non-righteous or unholy way. The word "just" means "*to be righteous.*" In the context of the verse above "just" (justice) can be equated to YEHOVAH's righteousness—His Holy Law. Therefore it is not our self-righteousness that brings the blessings of YEHOVAH upon our home, but rather we are blessed when we, in our hearts and actions, adhere to YEHOVAH's righteousness—His Torah, His Law, His instructions, and His Son Yehoshua.

Webster's dictionary defines a blessing as: *"the act or words of one that blesses"* and *"a thing conducive to happiness or welfare."* A curse is defined as: *"a cause of great harm or misfortune."* In ancient Hebrew times a "blessing" represented the favor of the person bestowing it and depending on that person's standing could be immensely valuable. This term is basically used in the same manner today. However, the term "curse" as it is used in the list of curses in Deuteronomy 28 is not as we commonly would understand it in the 21st century, i.e., as a gypsy curse of the evil eye, but rather as a way to describe a negative situation coming upon one as a consequence of their actions. Blessings were highly valued by the priests and people of the times, and curses avoided at all costs.

While both blessings and curses were a critical factor in ancient Hebrew times, most people today, considering themselves highly educated, discount the concept of curses and blessings. However, this system of reward and punishment was not put in place by YEHOVAH as an arbitrary or self-serving list of rules, but rather to guide the people into a way of living that would prosper them according to the natural and supernatural covenants of Elohim.

Of the many blessings and curses found in the Bible there are over 75 specific ones that relate to either the Creator's name or His Son's name. Some of these "blessing" verses could also be considered as promises—promises from YEHOVAH. We've included those verses as blessings since a promise from the Creator is one of the best blessings that a person could be given.

One of the first blessings found in the Bible is in Genesis 5:2. In this verse YEHOVAH blesses His creation with words that provide for their welfare and care in a supernatural way:

> Male and female created he them; and blessed them, and called their name Adam, in the day when they were created.
> GENESIS 5:2

Sadly, the very creatures who had been blessed by YEHOVAH on the day of their birth were deceived by the serpent and went on to disobey the single command Elohim gave them for their welfare—that they should not eat of the Tree of the Knowledge of Good and Evil. This resulted in the first recorded curse in the Bible:

> And YEHOVAH Elohim said unto the serpent, Because thou hast done this, thou *art* cursed above all cattle, and above every beast of the field; upon thy belly shalt thou

> go, and dust shalt thou eat all the days of thy life:
>
> GENESIS 3:14

The serpent's deception and Adam and Eve's lack of trust in YEHOVAH did not only bring repercussions on the serpent. Both Adam and Eve were cursed as well. Even though they had originally been created to live forever they became cursed to die because they chose to ignore YEHOVAH's warnings. Even worse, their disobedience rendered them spiritually dead—they and all their offspring relinquished their birthright to Satan. The good news is that YEHOVAH has redeemed us from Satan through the sacrifice of His son Yehoshua. However, it is still up to each of us to accept the gift of eternal life that Yehoshua's sacrifice offers us.

In addition to the curse of physical and spiritual death, Adam was sentenced to toil and labor to bring forth food from the earth whereas before it had grown with ease, and Eve would experience pain during childbirth whereas before there had been only joy. As their offspring we have inherited this curse and one day our bodies will also die. Unlike Adam and Eve who hid from the face of YEHOVAH after their fall from grace let us rather boldly seek the face of our Elohim. Let us count our blessings in this life and not take for granted the good things that YEHOVAH has bestowed upon us. Let us humble ourselves and realize that the blessings we have received from YEHOVAH can be lost if we allow Satan to deceive us. Yet, if we fail, forgiveness is available to us when we are contrite in heart, repent, and turn back to the Father as seen in II Chronicles where YEHOVAH provides a blessing within the following promise:

> If my people, which are called by my **name**, shall humble themselves, and pray, and seek my face, and turn from their wicked ways; then will I hear from heaven, and will forgive their sin, and will heal their land.
> II CHRONICLES 7:14

Repentance is important in our walk with YEHOVAH. The Messiah, through the power granted him by the Father, forgave sins but also told those he forgave to "go and sin no more." In fact, following the Father's example, Yehoshua told his disciples that they must forgive others as long as those they forgave also repented:

> Take heed to yourselves: If thy brother trespass against thee, rebuke him; and if he

repent, forgive him.

LUKE 17:3

Similar to the Father's desire to have His creation reconcile with Him, the Son went on to immediately add that should someone sin against them multiple times and then yet repent and ask forgiveness they must continue to forgive:

> And if he trespass against thee seven times in a day, and seven times in a day turn again to thee, saying, I repent; thou shalt forgive him.
>
> LUKE 17:4

Our Father will forgive us, if we accept the sacrifice of His son and repent (turn from our ways) and follow His ways—ways that will lead us to blessings. For those of us who do so YEHOVAH has released us from judgment as He did Israel even though they deserved judgment for rebelling against Him. He bore the shame of their rebellion and held His wrath to preserve His great name:

> For my **name's** sake will I defer mine anger, and for my praise will I refrain for thee, that

I cut thee not off.

ISAIAH 48:9

For His name's sake... what will we do to uphold the great and perfect name of YEHOVAH? Will we rebel against Him or repent and follow His ways? Many of the great prophets of the Bible sacrificed their will to YEHOVAH's will; some even sacrificed their lives.

Most people think of a prophet as someone who "sees the future." However, a Bible prophet was not a fortune-teller or a psychic reader. A true prophet's main focus was to bring Israel back into right relationship with their creator YEHOVAH. Yet before one rushes out and sign-up to be a prophet they should consider that a prophet must be exceedingly careful when speaking on behalf of YEHOVAH as shown in the following curse:

> But the prophet, which shall presume to speak a word in my name, which I have not commanded him to speak, or that shall speak in the name of other elohim, even that prophet shall die.
>
> DEUTERONOMY 18:20

Every true prophet of YEHOVAH was a mouthpiece of Elohim to the people. One of his responsibilities was to turn the people away from their sin by first making them aware of their transgressions—which they very rarely welcomed. Other Biblical patriarchs besides the prophets, such as Joshua, also had to deal with the people's strained relationship with the Creator:

> And if it seem evil unto you to serve YEHOVAH, choose you this day whom ye will serve; whether the elohim which your fathers served that *were* on the other side of the flood, or the elohim of the Amorites, in whose land ye dwell: but as for me and my house, we will serve YEHOVAH.
> JOSHUA 24:15

Strange as it might appear, some of the children of Israel allowed their carnal selves to lead them away from relationship with YEHOVAH to worship other elohim. Even though they were directly connected with historic biblical events such as the freedom from the bondage of Egypt, the manna coming down from heaven, and other sustaining miracles, they turned their back on YEHOVAH. This is evident in Joshua's admonition to the children of Israel in the following verse:

> Now therefore put away, *said he*, **the**

> **strange elohim which *are* among you**, and incline your heart unto YEHOVAH Elohim of Israel.
>
> JOSHUA 24:23

Perhaps the reason that their relationship with YEHOVAH was not as deeply important to them as we would imagine lies in the fact that the people themselves rejected a direct relationship with YEHOVAH. Gathered at the base of Mount Sinai they made the following request:

> And all the people saw the thunderings, and the lightnings, and the noise of the trumpet, and the mountain smoking: and when the people saw *it*, they removed, and stood afar off. And they said unto Moses, Speak thou with us, and we will hear: **but let not Elohim speak with us, lest we die**. And Moses said unto the people, Fear not: for Elohim is come to prove you, and that his fear may be before your faces, that ye sin not. And the people stood afar off, and Moses drew near unto the thick darkness where Elohim *was*. And YEHOVAH said unto Moses, Thus **thou shalt say** unto the

children of Israel, Ye have seen that I have talked with you from heaven.

EXODUS 20:18-22

The emphasis in the verse above has been added to make two points. First, as amazing as it sounds, the people themselves asked that the voice of YEHOVAH not be heard ever again by their ears. Can you imagine how tremendous the sounds and sensations must have been in order for them to make that request—to give up the direct experience of Elohim? Secondly, we see that Moses was instructed to speak the words of YEHOVAH to the people. The significance of that command is that since that very day at Mount Sinai to the present day, YEHOVAH has spoken through prophets to the people and not directly to His creation. Had the people never made this request we could very well be hearing YEHOVAH's voice today, in the same direct manner as the children of Israel experienced it long ago.

The greatest prophet, Messiah Yehoshua (Matt. 13:57, Mark 6:4), also came to restore the relationship of the people to YEHOVAH. He came to unburden them from the man-made laws and traditions that attempted to overrule the Creator's will. He came to free them so that they could fellowship with YEHOVAH as in the days of Adam and Eve before the fall from grace.

Blessings and Curses

In Yehoshua's name we find many biblical blessings, and as odd as this may sound, biblical curses as well. When most of us think of Yehoshua we only think of the attributes of peace and love, however consider the following verse:

> He that believeth on him is not condemned: but he that believeth not is **condemned already**, because he hath not believed in the name of the only begotten Son of Elohim.
> JOHN 3:18

Why is there a curse of condemnation associated with not believing on the name of Yehoshua? To answer this question let us examine the Messiah's relationship with YEHOVAH. What does YEHOVAH think of Yehoshua? The Word shows us. YEHOVAH makes his opinion of Yehoshua very clear during an event recorded in the Gospels known as the "transfiguration."

The transfiguration occurred during the festival of booths (YEHOVAH's feast of Sukkot). Peter and John are with Yehoshua who has taken them to the top of a mountain outside of Jerusalem. Then, to the disciples' amazement, the prophets Moses and Elijah suddenly appear alongside Yehoshua. They are bathed in a glorious light atop the mountain:

> While he [Peter] yet spake, behold, a bright cloud overshadowed them: and behold a voice out of the cloud, which said, This is my beloved Son, in whom I am well pleased; hear ye him.
>
> MATTHEW 17:5

There is no doubt from the verse above that Yehoshua was deep in YEHOVAH's favor; it is clear how YEHOVAH felt about His Son. And what did Yehoshua think of the Father? Yehoshua stated in John 10:30, *"I and my Father are one."* This verse shows that Yehoshua's will (the actions he took during his earthly life) was totally aligned with YEHOVAH's will. In other words, he did the work of the Father, and *only* those things that the Father showed him (John 5:19). He continues to do so today from his heavenly throne beside the Father.

Since Yehoshua's will is in alignment with the Father's will then it follows that if one rejects Yehoshua they are, in turn, rejecting YEHOVAH who sent him. If one rejects YEHOVAH then that person is cut-off (condemned).

The original covenant has many references to a person being "cut-off." Adam and Eve were cut-off as a result of their sin. Cain was cut-off and sentenced to wander the Earth because he murdered his brother Abel. The whole of humanity except for Noah and a handful of others were cut-off as a result of their choice to revel in evil-doing. If we find that we are cut-off it is up to each of us to reach out to our Father to restore the severed ties though His plan of redemption (the sacrifice of Yehoshua) and, like the prodigal son, return home in humility and love.

How can you gain the favor of YEHOVAH? Certainly by trusting in His Word but also by having an advocate. The Christian's advocate before YEHOVAH is Yehoshua—the Messiah of the Jews. When you ask something of the Father your request should be made in the name of one that the Father Himself favors; one that YEHOVAH knows by name—Yehoshua—in whom He is well pleased. The following blessing in the Messiah's name illustrates this point:

> Ye have not chosen me, but I have chosen you, and ordained you, that ye should go and bring forth fruit, and *that* your fruit should remain: that whatsoever ye shall ask of the Father in my name, he may give it you.
>
> JOHN 15:16

Yehoshua continues with another blessing later in this discourse informing his disciples that he will not directly intercede for them as a physical advocate in this world might, but rather it is their love for him and belief that YEHOVAH sent him that will serve as their advocate before Elohim. Therefore our love for Yehoshua is, in essence, our advocate before our Creator. And what is love? It is a choice we make:

> At that day ye shall ask **in my name**: and I say **not** unto you, that I will pray the Father for you: For the Father himself loveth you, because ye have loved me, and have believed that I came out from Elohim.
> JOHN 16:26-27

Like the prophets before him, Yehoshua came to point men and women back to the Father and to the Father's name. In examining the next verse it becomes clear that Yehoshua is stating that by declaring the name of YEHOVAH, the love Elohim gave to Yehoshua will also be given to us. This is a wonderful blessing that comes from the power of the name of our Elohim. Yehoshua also links his ability to reside in our hearts to the *outward* declaration of the name of YEHOVAH:

> And I have **declared** unto them **thy name**, and will **declare** *it*: that the love wherewith

thou hast loved me may be in them, **and I in them**.

> JOHN 17:26

Take a moment now to reflect on how important the name of our Elohim is to your spiritual welfare... What value do you place on YEHOVAH's holy name?

The actions taken by the Messiah on our behalf are not done to make a great name for himself. Yehoshua did not come for his own personal glory and fame (John 8:50). When Yehoshua was asked, "Good master, what shall I do to inherit eternal life?" he replied, "Why callest thou me good? None is good, save one, that is Elohim" (Luke 18:19). Yehoshua always deferred to the Father so that the Father would be glorified. The Messiah's example of humility is what we should strive to emulate in our lives.

The truth that Yehoshua taught in what is known as "The Lord's Prayer"—that all the glory and power belong to YEHOVAH—is also found in the following blessing/promise:

> And whatsoever ye shall ask in my name, that will I do, that the **Father** may be glorified in the Son.
>
> JOHN 14:13

In addition to Yehoshua's statements in the Gospels, other books of the new covenant contain blessings and curses. The next two references are taken from the book of Revelation. The first is both a curse and a blessing:

> And the nations were angry, and thy wrath is come, and the time of the dead, that they should be judged, and that thou shouldest give **reward** unto thy servants the prophets, and to the saints, and them that fear thy **name**, small and great; and shouldest **destroy** them which destroy the earth.
> REVELATION 11:18

Remember that another way to look at the meaning of "fear" is *to have profound adoring awed respect* for the object of the "fear." In this verse the object of "fear" is the name of Elohim. Since YEHOVAH is no respecter of persons (Acts 10:34-35), those both small and great, who have a *profound adoring awed respect* for the name of YEHOVAH will be given their reward, whereas those bringing death and destruction to the Earth will be cursed. And what will be their punishment—the result of their disobedience?

> And the smoke of their torment ascendeth up for ever and ever: and they have no rest day nor night, who worship the beast and his image, and whosoever receiveth the mark of his name.
>
> REVELATION 14:11

The last blessing and the last curse in the Bible are both found in the book of Revelation. These final verses illustrate a choice you must make. Will you give your allegiance to YEHOVAH or to others? These verses are also a reflection of an important choice put before the children of Israel in the original covenant's book of Deuteronomy as will be shown later:

Last Blessing in the Bible

> Blessed *are* they that do his commandments, that they may have right to the tree of life, and may enter in through the gates into the city.
>
> REVELATION 22:14

In this blessing Yehoshua is promising that those who follow the will of the Father can enter the gates of the new Jerusalem, to live in fellowship with him and the Father for eternity. The Tree of Life, which was once available for Adam and Eve to partake of in the garden, will be made available to the blessed ones who obey YEHOVAH's commands.

Interestingly, the verse in the original Greek contains the word *"plunontes"* which means to *"wash."* Most bibles actually translate the blessing as:

> Blessed are those who wash their robes, so that they may have the right to the tree of life, and may enter by the gates into the city.
> REVELATION 22:14 (NAS)

Washing is a symbol of purification known in Hebrew as the "mikvah," or in English: *"baptism."* When looking at this in context with other verses in Revelation, particularly Revelation 7:14, this purification is achieved by the washing of their robes in the blood of the lamb. Being baptized in the blood—the blood of Yehoshua—is what redeems and saves us from eternal separation from Elohim.

Last Curse in the Bible

> For I testify unto every man that heareth the words of the prophecy of this book, If any man shall add unto these things, Elo-

> him shall add unto him the plagues that are written in this book: And if any man shall take away from the words of the book of this prophecy, Elohim shall take away his part out of the book of life, and out of the holy city, and *from* the things which are written in this book.
>
> REVELATION 22:18-19

This final curse is of a type and style of a command found in the original covenant in the fifth book of Moses:

> Ye shall not add unto the word which I command you, neither shall ye diminish *ought* from it, that ye may keep the commandments of YEHOVAH your Elohim which I command you.
>
> DEUTERONOMY 4:2

In the verse above we are told to do only YEHOVAH's will. This is exactly what the Messiah did: his Father's will. But since Yehoshua had free will (like you and I have free will) he had to make a conscious choice to follow the Father's will. In the same way, you must choose whom you will follow. YEHOVAH gave all of us free will because, as much as He wants us to love, respect, and have fellowship with Him, He does not force us to do so—He wants us to desire it as well:

> Behold, I set before you this day a blessing and a curse; A blessing, if ye obey the commandments of YEHOVAH your Elohim, which I command you this day: and a curse, if ye will not obey the commandments of YEHOVAH your Elohim, but turn aside out of the way which I command you this day, to go after other elohim, which ye have not known.
> DEUTERONOMY 11:26-28

Some people may take these verses to mean that it is Elohim who lays the curse upon people. But it is not YEHOVAH who causes the effects of the curse to come upon people—no more than a loving Father would intentionally harm his own children. Rather, it is their choice to reject the Creator and His guidance (as given in His Word) that lays us open to Satan and his deceptions.

So which one will you choose? A world with Elohim and all the good that He is (Heaven) or a world separated from Elohim—from the source of all good—for where there is no good of any kind there is only evil (Hell).

Chapter 8

ISRAEL THE CHOSEN

> For thou *art* an holy people unto YEHOVAH thy Elohim, and YEHOVAH hath chosen thee to be a peculiar people unto himself, above all the nations that *are* upon the earth.
>
> DEUTERONOMY 14:2

How did Israel become YEHOVAH's chosen nation? The generally accepted answer to this question is "through the Abrahamic Covenant" (see Deut 7:7-8). However, In this chapter we will present an additional (perhaps even concurrent) possibility.

First, in order to answer this question we must look back in time to the days after the great flood. As the flood waters receded from the land, Noah and his wife, and their three sons; Ham, Shem, and Japheth and their wives left the ark and began resettling the Earth. They had been chosen by Elohim to be spared from the massive destruction because of Noah's righteousness before YEHOVAH.

Among these eight human beings and their offspring an event occurred that shaped the eventual creation of the nation of Israel. As recorded in Genesis chapter nine, Noah decided to plant a vineyard. After a hard day of work tilling the fields he retired to his tent and drank some wine. His labors must have been great as he actually became drunk and passed out. One of his sons, Ham, either was looking for his father or perhaps was with him drinking and "saw his father's nakedness." Later, after leaving the tent Ham told his brothers what he "saw." Shem and Japheth then covered Noah with a robe by backing into Noah's tent, not looking at Noah directly:

> And Shem and Japheth took a garment, and laid *it* upon both their shoulders, and went backward, and covered the nakedness of their father; and their faces *were* backward, and they saw not their father's nakedness.
>
> GENESIS 9:23

But when Noah awoke and learned what Ham had "done" he was very upset. Bible scholars and readers have varying opinions on what Ham actually had "done" to his father. For if Ham had accidentally seen his father naked in the tent because his father fell asleep drunk then the next act that Noah takes makes little sense:

> And Noah awoke from his wine, and knew what his younger son had done unto him. And he said, Cursed *be* Canaan; a servant of servants shall he be unto his brethren. And he said, Blessed *be* YEHOVAH, Elohim of Shem; and Canaan shall be his servant.
> GENESIS 9:24-26

What had Ham done that was deserving of such a fierce curse? Some say that Ham may have had sexual relations with his father as the term "saw" his nakedness and "uncovered" his nakedness are similar. The act of "uncovering" someone's nakedness as used in the original testament is a euphemism for having sexual relations with someone. Others say that Ham may have had relations with Noah's wife and that Ham's son Canaan was the illegitimate offspring. Either of these acts would have been cause for the harsh curse imposed by Noah. It also must have been a righteous curse as the Bible states that a curse that has no foundation will not land on one:

> As the bird by wandering, as the swallow

> by flying, so the curse causeless shall not come.
>
> PROVERBS 26:2

The blessing and curse in Genesis 9:24-26 spoken by Noah, a man highly favored by YEHOVAH, would travel down the years (as we shall show) all the way to Shem's descendant, Abraham, to be completely fulfilled:

> In the same day YEHOVAH made a covenant with Abram, saying, Unto thy seed have I given this land, from the river of Egypt unto the great river, the river Euphrates:
>
> GENESIS 15:18

The true boundaries of the land that YEHOVAH set aside for the seed of Abraham are far greater than the amount of land that the state of Israel currently controls. The boundaries of the promised land as specified by YEHOVAH stretch from the Nile river on the west to the Euphrates river in the middle of Iraq on the east and encompasses all of Syria, all of Jordan, and about half of Saudi Arabia. As mentioned, Israel does not have full possession of the promised land yet. However, rather than expand its borders, Israel is currently being pressured into *giving up* the little land

Israel the Chosen

they do have.

Why do we say only the children of Israel are to inherit the land and not the other tribes descended from Ishmael—who are also the seed of Abraham (the Arabs)? This is because YEHOVAH made it clear to Abraham that it would be through the seed of Isaac, Abraham's yet unborn son with Sarah, that the covenant would be fulfilled:

> And Abraham said unto Elohim, O that Ishmael might live before thee! And Elohim said, Sarah thy wife shall bear thee a son indeed; and thou shalt call his name Isaac: and I will establish my covenant with him [Isaac] for an everlasting covenant, *and* with his seed after him.
> GENESIS 17:18-19

Continuing down the generations we find that Isaac had two sons; Esau and Jacob. Esau, the firstborn, sold his birthright/inheritance to his twin brother as seen in Genesis 25:31-33. But it wasn't until Isaac's deathbed blessing (intended for the first-born Esau) was bestowed on Jacob that the covenant would continue through Jacob's seed and not Esau's. In the following verse Isaac is speaking to Jacob whom he believes is Esau:

> Let people serve thee, and nations bow down to thee: be master over thy brethren, and let thy mother's sons bow down to thee: cursed *be* every one that curseth thee, and blessed *be* he that blesseth thee.
>
> GENESIS 27:29

When Esau learned that Jacob had impersonated him in order to receive their father's blessing he pleaded with his father to bless him also. Isaac, even though he loved Esau greater, would not grant his son's request. His word had already been spoken—his blessing given. By not retracting his blessing, Isaac emulated Elohim—for once spoken, YEHOVAH's words and covenants are unbreakable and irrevocable. Isaac's blessing therefore sealed the transfer of the covenant between YEHOVAH and himself to YEHOVAH and his son Jacob. YEHOVAH later confirms this directly with Jacob:

> And, behold, YEHOVAH stood above it, and said, I *am* YEHOVAH, Elohim of Abraham thy father, and the Elohim of Isaac: the land whereon thou liest, to thee will I give it, and to thy seed: And thy seed shall be as the dust of the earth, and thou shalt spread abroad to the west, and to the east, and to

Israel the Chosen

the north, and to the south: and in thee and in thy seed shall all the families of the earth be blessed.

GENESIS 28: 13-14

Jacob went on to have twelve sons: Reuben, Simeon, Levi, Judah, Zebulun, Issachar, Dan, Ga_, Asher, Naphtali, Joseph, and Benjamin. As seen in an earlier chapter Jacob received a new name from Elohim. After wrestling with the Creator for a full night Jacob was renamed Israel, which means "*he who has striven (isra) with Elohim (el).*" Therefore, his twelve sons are known as the twelve tribes of Israel (*isra-el*).

Joseph, the most beloved son of Israel (Jacob) became one of the most powerful persons in the entire world when he saved Egypt from certain destruction through the interpretation of Pharaoh's dream. Through favor and reward, Joseph was given some of the most fertile land in Egypt, called the Goshen. His father, and his brothers, and family and flocks fled the great famine of the times and settled in Goshen with Joseph.

Over many years they grew into a great multitude and were an honored people in the land. However, other Pharaohs, who came later, forgot the past contributions of the Hebrews and enslaved the children of Israel. The children of Israel toiled many more years under their Egyptian taskmasters until Moses was called to lead them to freedom in the promised land:

> And YEHOVAH said, I have surely seen the affliction of **my people** which *are* in Egypt, and have heard their cry by reason of their taskmasters; for I know their sorrows;
>
> EXODUS 3:7

YEHOVAH heard the cry of His people. Even though all of creation was YEHOVAH's possession, including the Egyptians, Elohim called out the children of Israel as "my people." This proves that a special relationship exists between them—they are His chosen people. However it is not because of the people's greatness that YEHOVAH favored them but because of the covenant He made with their forefathers:

> YEHOVAH did not set his love upon you, nor choose you, because ye were more in number than any people; for ye *were* the fewest of all people: But because YEHOVAH loved you, and because he would keep the oath which he had sworn unto your fathers, hath YEHOVAH brought you out with a mighty hand, and redeemed you out of the house of bondmen, from the

> hand of Pharaoh king of Egypt.
> DEUTERONOMY 7: 7-8

Through the power of YEHOVAH and the mighty deeds He brought to bear against the empire of Egypt, the children of Israel were freed from bondage. Moses led them out of Egypt with great wealth (given to them by the Egyptian people—see Exodus 12:35-36) and headed out across the desert to the promised land. Once there, however, they could not simply take possession of the land. They first had to drive out the inhabitants.

One of the main tribes that lived in the land was the Canaanites, who are considered to be the descendants of Canaan, the son of Ham. Because of their detestable practices—that included the worship of graven images—YEHOVAH commanded the children of Israel to remove the Canaanites from the land. Our Mighty Elohim supernaturally assisted the Israelites as they battled against the Canaanites and other tribes in the land including the Philistines, Moabites, Edomites, Hittites, and Ammonites.

Thus, through the actions of the seed of Abraham (Isaac and Jacob), the curse of Noah upon Canaan, son of Ham, as outlined in our scenario, was finally fulfilled. The children of Israel defeated the cursed Canaanites and took possession of the land. The Hebrews called their new nation the nation of Israel—the only nation actually decreed into existence by the Creator—its boundaries specifically called out by He who made the entire Earth:

> And what one nation in the earth *is* like thy people, *even* like Israel, whom Elohim went to redeem for a people to himself, and to **make him a name**, and to do for you great things and terrible, for thy land, before thy people, which thou redeemedst to thee from Egypt, *from* the nations and their elohim?
> II SAMUEL 7:23

A special blessing was even given for YEHOVAH's chosen called the "Aaronic blessing." At the end of this special blessing Elohim links His name to the blessing and to the people of Israel:

> And they [Aaron and his sons] shall put **my name** upon the children of Israel; and I will bless them.
> NUMBERS 6:27

Contrary to the teaching of some denominations that the church has replaced Israel as Elohim's chosen, the Word states that YEHOVAH is Elohim of Israel forever:

> And yet for all that, when they be in the land of their enemies, I will not cast them away, neither will I abhor them, to destroy them utterly, and to break my covenant with them: for I *am* YEHOVAH their Elohim. But I will for their sakes remember the covenant of their ancestors, whom I brought forth out of the land of Egypt in the sight of the heathen, that I might be their Elohim: I *am* YEHOVAH.
>
> LEVITICUS 26:44-45

The Creator is all-powerful. Yet we believe He has not given Himself the power to go against His own Word. The agreements and covenants that He has made (and will make) do not limit His power, but rather they limit the choices He allows Himself to make. Keeping His Word and His covenants is a sign of His honor. The Creator's Word binds Him and so should ours. Consider the following verse from the book of Job:

> Knowest thou the ordinances of heaven? Canst thou set the dominion thereof in the

> earth?
>
> JOB 38:33

The Creator is pointing out to Job that Job isn't aware of the laws (ordinances) governing Heaven. These laws are the spoken Word of the Creator. Could it be that there are other ordinances in force, perhaps with the angelic beings (the obedient and the fallen) that we know nothing about—which are also in effect right now? When we throw our hands up, prostrate ourselves on the ground and state that the Creator "works in mysterious ways" perhaps the mysterious part is that we don't know all the laws and covenants He has previously made that are currently in force.

The Creator's covenant with the children of Israel is forever. Even though Israel has repeatedly broken their agreements, Elohim does not abandon nor will He ever abandon His chosen people. If He broke His Word—the Word that created the universe (Genesis 1:3)—the very fabric of life as we know it could unravel. Therefore, we can assuredly trust the Word of the Creator to guide our choices in life.

The covenants of YEHOVAH are eternal, and by His own Word they last forever. We trust in Him and His word, and we glorify His name forever. As the Psalmist wrote, the children of Israel did the same:

> Some *trust* in chariots, and some in horses: but we will **remember the name of YEHOVAH** our Elohim.
>
> PSALMS 20:7

Not the title "the LORD," or the name G_d, but only the name of our Creator. Yet, even though Israel had the favor of YEHOVAH, over time they turned their back on Him. In the book of Kings we read how some kings of Israel honored YEHOVAH and obeyed His commandments while other kings of Israel disregarded His covenant and commandments. When Israel disobeyed and turned away from YEHOVAH, Israel's enemies overcame her. But righteous men of the nation called on the name of YEHOVAH to reconcile the people with their mighty Elohim:

> Remember me, O YEHOVAH, with the favor *that thou bearest unto* thy people: O visit me with thy salvation; that I may see the good of **thy chosen**, that I may rejoice in the gladness of **thy nation**, that I may glory with **thine inheritance**. We have sinned with our fathers, we have committed iniquity, we have done wickedly. Our fathers understood not thy wonders in Egypt; they remembered not the multitude of thy mer-

cies; but provoked *him* at the sea, *even* at the Red sea. Nevertheless he [YEHOVAH] saved them for **his name's sake**, that he might make his mighty power to be known.
PSALMS 106:4-8

The children of Israel are under pressure today by all the nations of the Earth to relinquish their inheritance. Just as in days long ago when the enemies of Israel hated her name and came against her with a vengeance, so too now are all nations aligning themselves against Israel. The following verse from the book of Psalms, written over 2500 years ago, could easily be found in a newspaper today:

They have said, Come, and let us cut them off from *being* a nation; that the **name** of Israel may be no more in remembrance.
PSALMS 83:4

Israel's enemies have come close to achieving their goal many times throughout history. The children of Israel were dispersed (exiled) among the nations after the destruction of Jerusalem and the second temple in A.D. 70. However, for the first time in history a nation that had been "extinct" for over 2000 years became a nation again. On May 14th, 1948, only

Israel the Chosen

three short years after the end of the holocaust (that had decimated over six million of their brethren), Israel was declared a nation. Israel's historic declaration ends with:

> Placing our trust in the Almighty, we affix our signatures to this proclamation at this session of the provisional council of state, on the soil of the Homeland, in the city of Tel-Aviv, on this Sabbath eve, the 5th day of Iyar, 5708 (14th May, 1948).

On the very same day that the nation of Israel was reborn (May 14th, 1948) it was attacked. The surrounding Arab countries of Egypt, Iraq, Syria, Jordan, Lebanon, and Saudi Arabia joined forces in an effort to fulfill the fourth verse of Psalm 83. Even though Israel had only one tank to defend herself against a well-armed combined enemy force she defeated her attackers and even enlarged her borders. Against all odds Israel prevailed. Surely the supernatural hand of YEHOVAH was upon Israel.

In 1967 a second war erupted with even more countries aligned against Israel. Despite overwhelming odds Israel arose victoriously and once again gained more land including the holy city of Jerusalem, which is home to the sacred site of the first and second temples known as the Temple Mount.

The third major conflict between Israel and the surrounding Arab nations during the modern era was a surprise attack against Israel by many of the same countries involved in the 1967 war. The attack began on October 6th, 1973, on Yom Kippur—the Day of Atonement (the holiest day of the year for the Jewish people) when nearly all of Israel was at the synagogues, fasting and praying as commanded by YEHOVAH in Leviticus 16:29-30.

Despite Israel's enemies having the element of surprise and the fact that the Israeli forces were in a state of disarray, within three weeks the Israelis had pushed back the invaders and enlarged their territory once again. The Israeli forces were only 62 miles from the capital of Egypt and within 24 miles of the capital of Syria, when, fearing complete loss, the Arabian attackers pleaded for peace. Only twenty days after the conflict began it ended.

Israel, a tiny nation slightly smaller than New Jersey (only 1/640th the landmass of its Arab enemies) had overcome a combined force that should have prevailed against them each time. YEHOVAH, the Mighty One of Israel, defended His chosen people in each of these wars just as He had done in Israel's Biblical past. He still defends them today, and will do so again in the prophetic future:

> Behold, I [YEHOVAH] will make Jerusalem a cup of trembling unto all the people round about, when they shall be in the siege both against Judah *and* against Jerusalem. And in that day will I make Jerusalem a burdensome stone for all people: all that burden themselves with it shall be cut in pieces, though **all the people of the earth** be gathered together against it. In that day, saith YEHOVAH, I will smite every horse with astonishment, and his rider with madness: and I will open mine eyes upon the house of Judah, and will smite every horse of the people with blindness.
>
> ZECHARIAH 12:2-4

The nations know not against whom they rail. They believe they are going against only flesh and blood when in reality they are going against the Creator of the entire universe.

> Look unto me, and be ye saved, all the ends of the earth: for I *am* Elohim, and *there is* none else. I have sworn by myself, the word is gone out of my mouth *in* righteousness, and shall not return, that unto me **every** knee shall bow, **every** tongue shall swear.

> Surely, shall *one* say, in YEHOVAH have I righteousness and strength: *even* to him shall *men* come; and all that are incensed against him shall be ashamed.
>
> ISAIAH 45: 22-24

As the end of this present age approaches, all nations are currently aligning themselves against Israel, just as predicted in the Bible. With no one to defend them except YEHOVAH, Israel will triumph over those who would kill them and in the process blot out their enemies' names from remembrance.

Israel will once again return to fully trust in YEHOVAH and will come to know that YEHOVAH is their Elohim, and that Yehoshua is their Messiah. Just as Elohim made His name great by redeeming His chosen people from the bondage of slavery in Egypt over 3000 years ago, He will demonstrate the greatness of His name again. He will rescue His people Israel from certain destruction and all mankind will proclaim that the name of the great and mighty Elohim of ALL creation is none other than YEHOVAH.

> Father, glorify thy name. Then came there a voice from heaven, *saying*, I have both glorified *it*, and will glorify *it* again.
>
> JOHN 12:28

Chapter 9

THE PROPHECY OF HOSEA

> And Elohim **said**, Let there be light: and there was light.
>
> GENESIS 1:3

Consider for a moment how everything that you experience, even the very air that you breathe and the light that illuminates the Earth was SPOKEN into existence by YEHOVAH. For example, when Elohim said *"let there be light"* there was light (Genesis 1:3). How very important and powerful then must be the spoken words of an anointed prophet who has been called by YEHOVAH to be His mouthpiece:

> And I [YEHOVAH] have put my words in thy mouth, and I have covered thee in the shadow of mine hand, that I may plant the heavens, and lay the foundations of the earth, and say unto Zion, Thou *art* my people.
>
> ISAIAH 51:16

Hosea was one such anointed prophet who was called to be the voice of YEHOVAH to the children of Israel. The name Hosea is pronounced "Ho-*shea*." It means "*salvation*" and is very similar to Yehoshua's name which means "*YEHOVAH is salvation.*" Hosea's name most likely was given to him by YEHOVAH as the book of Hosea paints a historic and prophetic picture of the rebellion and ultimate salvation of the children of Israel.

Hosea served YEHOVAH during the reign of the Judean kings Uzziah, Jotham, Ahaz, Hezekiah, and Jeroboam, spanning the years from approximately 790 B.C. to at least 722 B.C. Historically, this time period was marked by a steep political decline and increasing moral degradation, eventually resulting in Israel's fall to Assyria. According to the book of Hosea the downfall of the nation is attributed to the people's worship of other elohim. This is a grave sin, a violation of the first and most important commandment:

> Thou shalt have none other elohim before me.
>
> DEUTERONOMY 5:7

And yet the people honored and sacrificed to other elohim as seen in the following verse:

> And I will visit upon her the days of Baalim, wherein she burned incense to them, and she decked herself with her earrings and her jewels, and she went after her lovers [the Ba_ls], and **forgat me**, saith YEHOVAH.
>
> HOSEA 2:13

"Ba_ls" (plural for Ba_l) is the collective name of the many ancient Phoenician sex/fertility idols that were worshiped by the tribes of Israel during Hosea's lifetime and beyond. "Ba_l" is translated as "Lord" in English.[1]

Calling our Creator "the LORD" and addressing our Messiah as "Lord" is *not* the will of our heavenly Father, for several reasons. First and foremost the phrase "the Lord" is *not* the name of the Father nor the Son. Second, it is derived from *Ba_l*, a false elohim.[2] Therefore using the word "Lord" when addressing YEHOVAH could be considered the same as calling Him by the name of another elohim; the worship of which provoked the wrath of YEHOVAH during Hosea's time period and resulted in the fall of Israel:

> Therefore I [YEHOVAH] have hewed by prophets, I have slain them by sayings of

> My mouth, And My judgments to the light goeth forth.
>
> HOSEA 6:5 (YLT)

To show you just how abhorrent the name Ba_l is, consider that the name of the demon Be_lzebub (Ba'_l z_bub) is also derived from Ba_l!

Oh how weak is the flesh that even YEHOVAH's chosen ones succumbed to their fallen sin nature and turned their back on their Elohim. They grieved YEHOVAH's heart over and over again as they betrayed the vow they made to Him at the base of Mount Sinai—where they had agreed to obey His commandments and to be a nation of priests.

> ...*there is* none among them that calleth unto me.
>
> HOSEA 7:7

Throughout the book of Hosea YEHOVAH tells His people how much He loves them and wishes to show them mercy and kindness, and how He'd prefer that they *know* Him (His name, His true nature, His abiding love) rather than treating Him as a Lord who needs to be appeased by burnt offerings:

> For I [YEHOVAH] desired mercy, and not

> sacrifice; and the **knowledge** of Elohim more than burnt offerings.
>
> HOSEA 6:6

YEHOVAH so loves His chosen people Israel that although they transgress over and over again, if they repent and seek His face by calling on *His* name, He will forgive them. Yet He also must chastise them (like a father must do to his children) when they refuse to listen to His holy ordinances and do not seek His presence. YEHOVAH makes it clear that He does not desire this chastisement; He would rather show them mercy and loving kindness.

YEHOVAH makes His will known not only by the spoken words of the prophets; He will sometimes require His prophets to act outwardly in strange manners in order to demonstrate His will to the people and to lead them back to the covenant. For example, YEHOVAH ordered Ezekiel to bear the iniquity (lawlessness) of Israel by lying on his side for many days as the nation watched in perplexity:

> Lie thou also upon thy left side, and lay the iniquity of the house of Israel upon it: *according* to the number of the days that thou shalt lie upon it thou shalt bear their iniquity. For I [YEHOVAH] have laid upon

> thee the years of their iniquity, according to the number of the days, three hundred and ninety days: so shalt thou bear the iniquity of the house of Israel.
>
> EZEKIEL 4:4-5

And what strange thing, if any, did YEHOVAH require of Hosea? Contrary to what we would expect as a moral choice for a chosen prophet, YEHOVAH commanded Hosea to take a prostitute for a wife:

> ...and YEHOVAH said to Hosea, Go, take unto thee a wife of whoredoms and children of whoredoms: for the land hath committed great whoredom, *departing* from YEHOVAH.
>
> HOSEA 1:2

Why would YEHOVAH make such an unusual request? This is because YEHOVAH wants to have Hosea teach the people not only through words, but also by the example of his life. So like Ezekiel, Hosea obeys the Father. He takes the prostitute Gomer to be his wife as the people watch in bewilderment.

Hosea goes on to have several children by Gomer. Each child is given a specific name that indicates YEHOVAH's displeasure with the actions of Israel as well as a prophetic warning of the judgment that will be coming against them. The first child born to Hosea and Gomer was named "Jezreel."

> And YEHOVAH said unto him [Hosea], Call his name Jezreel; for yet a little *while*, and I will avenge the blood of Jezreel upon the house of Jehu, and will cause to cease the kingdom of the house of Israel. And it shall come to pass at that day, that I will break the bow of Israel in the valley of Jezreel.
>
> HOSEA 1:4-5

The name Jezreel means *"Elohim will scatter."* Through this name YEHOVAH warns Israel of the consequences of their behavior—that the royal line of Israel's kings will fall and the people will be dispersed and scattered. It's interesting to note that the name Jezreel has endured to this day in that the Jezreel valley, located in the northern part of Israel, has often been the site of many bloody battles, and it is predicted to be the future site of the Battle of Armageddon in end-times prophecy.

Predictably, Gomer proves to be unfaithful to Hosea; she is sexually intimate with other men, and is even believed to have had children with other men.

Most scholars agree that their next two children named Loruhamah and Loammi, were probably conceived in adultery and were not even Hosea's natural children. Note again the emphasis on the meaning of the names YEHOVAH gives to their children:

> And she [Gomer] conceived again, and bare a daughter. And *Elohim* said unto him, Call her name Loruhamah: for I will no more have mercy upon the house of Israel; but I will utterly take them away.
> HOSEA 1:6

Loruhamah's name means *"not pitied, not having obtained mercy."* This name contains a prophetic warning of YEHOVAH's disapproval and eventual withdrawal from the people as a consequence of their sin and their breaking of the covenant they made with Him.

YEHOVAH's intent to withdraw the hand of His protection is clear—for their next child is named Loammi which means *"not my people."*

> Now when she had weaned Loruhamah, she conceived, and bare a son. Then said *Elohim*, Call his name Loammi for ye *are*

not my people, and I will not be your *Elohim*.

HOSEA 1:8-9

Gomer eventually abandons Hosea and leaves him completely for other lovers, not appreciating his goodness, kindness, and love. Israel, like Gomer, had *committed great whoredom*:

> And she [Israel] shall follow after her lovers, but she shall not overtake them; and she shall seek them, but shall not find *them*: then shall she say, I will go and return to my first husband; for then *was it* better with me than now. For she did not know that I [YEHOVAH] gave her corn, and wine, and oil, and multiplied her silver and gold, *which* they prepared for Baal [the Lord]. Therefore will I return, and take away my corn in the time thereof, and my wine in the season thereof, and will recover my wool and my flax *given* to cover her nakedness.
> HOSEA 2:7-9

Israel behaved like a prostitute; they worshipped many other elohim, and turned away from their Creator, YEHOVAH, the same way Gomer turned to other men. This is why YEHOVAH commanded Hosea to marry a prostitute—so that by Hosea's actions, YEHOVAH could paint a living picture of how Israel had treated their Elohim.

In Hosea 2:7-9 above YEHOVAH is saying that no matter how much Israel seeks after her false idols she shall not find them, for all along while they were offering gifts to the false elohim Ba_l it had been YEHOVAH who had taken care of them, providing them with their corn, silver, etc. To teach them He had to first chastise them by taking away all that He had provided them. Only then would they choose to return to Him. Similarly, Hosea's adulterous wife returned to him when she realized he had taken better care of her than her lovers had.

The consequences for Israel's covenant-breaking idolatry is clear:

> My people are destroyed for lack of **knowledge**: because thou hast rejected knowledge, I will also reject thee, that thou shalt be no priest to me: seeing thou hast forgotten the law of thy Elohim, I will also forget thy children.
>
> HOSEA 4:6

Knowledge of what? Of YEHOVAH's Word—which

is righteousness. However, YEHOVAH still loves His people and provides a way for reconciliation. On the day that Israel stops calling Him Ba_lim, and begins calling Him by His rightful name and obeying His commands, He will make a new covenant with them, and nothing will hurt them evermore:

> **For I will take away the names of Baalim out of her mouth**, and they shall no more be remembered by their **name**. And in that day will I make a covenant for them with the beasts of the field, and with the fowls of heaven, and *with* the creeping things of the ground: and I will break the bow and the sword and the battle out of the earth, and will make them to lie down safely.
> HOSEA 2:17-18

These verses are believed to foretell the millennial period of peace that will come to the Earth after the Jews recognize that Yehoshua, the son of YEHOVAH, is their Messiah. They will come to know YEHOVAH as He really is, full of love, mercy and affection. They will see that it is YEHOVAH who provides for their every need like a husband would for his wife:

> And it shall be at that day, saith YEHOVAH,

> *that* thou shalt call me Ishi [husband]; and shalt call me no more Baali [Lord].
>
> HOSEA 2:16

It should be clear now that our Creator does not want to be called by the name of false elohim, nor does He want to be called by the English translated version of Ba_l—"the Lord" which according to Webster means 1: *a ruler or master,* 2: *the head of a feudal state,* 3: *a titled nobleman.* YEHOVAH made it clear that He does not want a relationship based on that of a dictator to a subject, rather He wants His people to know Him, to be on intimate, affectionate terms with Him, to call on Him by name and not by a title that implies distance or authoritative control.

For example, while Queen Elizabeth may require her subjects to address her as "her Royal Highness" or "her Majesty," this is not what our Creator desires. He wants to be family. He wants the closeness that is invoked by the words, "this is YEHOVAH, my husband (Ishi), my wonderful provider, the head of my household, the one I look to for my every need." He wants us to commune and confer with Him every day, just as we would normally do with our husband or our wife:

> And I [YEHOVAH] will betroth thee [Israel] unto me for ever; yea, I will betroth thee

> unto me in righteousness, and in judgment, and in loving kindness, and in mercies. I will even betroth thee unto me in faithfulness: and thou shalt **know** YEHOVAH.
>
> HOSEA 2:19-20

While the book of Hosea is in essence a story of how our heavenly Father honors His covenants with long-suffering patience, preferring mercy over chastisement, and ultimate forgiveness for His chosen people; Hosea's words also speak prophetically to present-day believers—for they contain shadow pictures of YEHOVAH's ultimate gift to Israel and to every believer; the gift of salvation and eternal life through the redemptive sacrifice of His only begotten Son: Yehoshua.

> After two days will he revive us: in the third day he will raise us up, and we shall live in his sight.
>
> HOSEA 6:2

> Then shall we know, *if* we follow on to **know** YEHOVAH: his going forth is prepared as the morning; and he shall come unto us as the rain, as the latter *and* former rain unto the earth.
>
> HOSEA 6:3

Just as Israel depended upon the rains for their very lives (without rain the land of Israel was barren and could produce no fruit) so too was Yehoshua sent as both the latter and the former rain, whose Word, life, and resurrection provides every believer with both the way to know YEHOVAH as well as the ultimate gift of forgiveness from sin. In this way Yehoshua is the rain (grace) that enables each of us to produce fruit for the glory of Elohim.

Let all believers rejoice that YEHOVAH is a covenant-keeping Elohim, whose mighty Word promises that He will answer our prayers:

> And it hath come to pass in that day, I answer—an affirmation of YEHOVAH, I answer the heavens, and they answer the earth.
>
> HOSEA 2:21 (YLT)

Let us not continue in the tradition of the people of Hosea's time who turned their back on YEHOVAH and called upon the false elohim Ba_l. Let us accept YEHOVAH as He would have us accept Him—as husband (Ishi) to beloved wife.

Chapter 10

KEEPING THE NAME PURE

> Speak unto Aaron and to his sons, that they separate themselves from the holy things of the children of Israel, and that they profane not my holy name *in those things* which they hallow unto me: I *am* YEHOVAH.
>
> LEVITICUS 22:2

Webster defines "profane" as *"to treat something sacred with abuse, irreverence, or contempt."* In the verses above YEHOVAH commands the priests of Israel to treat His set-apart name with reverence and love. The command to treat the Name appropriately appears to be self-evident, for who among us, especially our priests and ministers, would choose to profane Elohim? Yet our fallen human nature requires continual reinforcement to keep the flesh and mind in line with the intent of the spirit within us.

The word "hallow" is rarely used in conversation today. Its meaning is *"to set apart for holy use."* The term "holy" is an adjective that means, in part, *"devoted entirely to the deity or work of the deity."* Therefore YEHOVAH is explaining to the priests that He will be holy amongst the people of Israel, and that it is He, YEHOVAH, who sets them apart for holy use—His use. The ministry was not created for the priests and ministers to do their own will. It was created to do Elohim's will. And how do they know His will? From the Word—all of it.

You may say that since Leviticus 22:2 applies to the priestly class why should those of us who are not ministers, reverends, priests, or Levites concern ourselves with it? Yehoshua taught that unless our righteousness exceeds that of the scribes and the Pharisees we would not see the kingdom of Heaven (Matthew 5:20). The scribes and Pharisees followed the letter of the law, but we are also commanded to follow the spirit of the law. Should we aim for anything less?

For those who believe that we are under grace and that the Messiah's sacrifice has paid for all our sin; past, present, and future we say: Yes, that is true. If we accept Yehoshua then he will stand before the Father on judgment day to declare that we are one of His own. But this does not give believers a license to sin.

Even though Yehoshua never sinned he knew the dangers of sin, in fact, after one miracle healing he said to the healed man, *"Behold, thou art made whole:*

sin no more, lest a worse thing come unto thee" (John 5:14). He also told the woman who had been caught in the act of adultery "*Neither do I condemn thee: go, and sin no more*" (John 8:11). You see, just like an earthly father forgives and teaches the right way of living to his sons and daughters, our heavenly Father does the same.

In the following verses YEHOVAH, through the prophet Isaiah, is speaking to those priests whose hearts were not pure as they performed the duties and the sacrifices of the original covenant. Similar to Yehoshua's admonition that we must go a level deeper in order to reach Heaven, YEHOVAH proclaims that all who follow the law outwardly but do not hear His voice when He calls will have their "*fears come upon them.*"

> He that killeth an ox *is* as *if* he slew a man; he that sacrificeth a lamb, as *if* he cut off a dog's neck; he that offereth an oblation, as *if he offered* swine's blood; he that burneth incense, *as if* he blessed an idol. Yea, they have chosen their own ways, and their soul delighteth in their abominations. I [YEHOVAH] also will choose their delusions, and will bring their fears upon them; because when I called, none did answer; when I spake, they did not hear: but they

did evil before mine eyes, and chose *that* in which I delighted not.

ISAIAH 66:3-4

Abomination is a very strong word. Once again, it is a word that is seldom used in conversation today but it is found many times in the Bible. It means *"extreme disgust and hatred"* for the object of the abomination. YEHOVAH considers the "righteous" acts of a man an abomination if his heart is not pure. These men, as Yehoshua stated in Matthew 23:27 are hypocrites who on the outside are as whited sepulchers that have a clean appearance yet inside they are as rotted bones. Similarly, if your good works are performed with a heart not surrendered to Elohim then you are like those who sacrificed in a ritualistic manner while their hearts were not true to YEHOVAH.

If your heart's intent is to love YEHOVAH then you will follow His commands to the best of your ability each day. As Yehoshua said:

If ye love me, keep my commandments.

JOHN 14:15

And what are Yehoshua's commands? Consider first that Yehoshua always did the will of the Father. He himself stated, *"I and the Father are one"* (John

10:30), i.e., their will is one as when two people say they "are of one mind." Therefore the "my commandments" referred to in John 14:15 are YEHOVAH's commandments.

In Matthew 22:37-40 the Messiah summarized all of the commandments into two main ones:

> Yehoshua said unto him, Thou shalt love YEHOVAH thy Elohim with all thy heart, and with all thy soul, and with all thy mind. This is the first and great commandment. And the second *is* like unto it, Thou shalt love thy neighbor as thyself. On these two commandments hang all the law and the prophets.
>
> MATTHEW 22:37-40

Some denominations claim that since we are under grace our actions do not matter. If this is true then why follow Yehoshua's commands or for that matter any of YEHOVAH's commandments? The answer is "because we love them" (John 14:15).

The actions we take and the intent of our heart matters today just as in the days of ancient Israel. When we first began an in-depth study of the Bible and the Hebrew roots of Christianity, we were surprised to learn that the children of Israel continued to disobey

YEHOVAH even after they were reprimanded for worshiping a golden calf at the base of Mount Sinai:

> When thou art come into the land which YEHOVAH thy Elohim giveth thee, thou shalt not learn to do after the abominations of those nations.
> DEUTERONOMY 18:9

Even though they were commanded by Elohim to not learn the ways of the pagans—ways that would pollute them (and by association pollute the Creator's name)—they did so anyway. They worshipped other elohim and even sacrificed their children to a false deity—throwing them into a fiery furnace in the belly of an idol:

> And thou shalt not let any of thy seed pass through *the fire* to Molech; neither shalt thou profane **the name** of thy Elohim; I *am* YEHOVAH.
> LEVITICUS 18:21

One might expect the people to succumb to false idols but what about the priests of Israel? Did they ever profane YEHOVAH's holy name?

Keeping the Name Pure

> They [priests] shall be holy unto their Elohim, and not profane **the name** of their Elohim: for the offerings of YEHOVAH made by fire, *and* the bread of their Elohim, they do offer: therefore they shall be holy.
>
> LEVITICUS 21:6

Unfortunately they did sin against YEHOVAH. Just as the children of Israel turned their back on their Elohim so too did the priests of Israel:

> Then he brought me to the door of the gate of YEHOVAH's house which *was* toward the north; and, behold, there sat women weeping for Tammuz.
>
> EZEKIEL 8:14

The word T_m_uz is currently the name of the 4th month of the Hebrew year (the 10th month on the Jewish civil calendar). However, this was not always so. The name T_m_uz was adopted from the Babylonian calendar during the Jewish captivity in Babylon (approximately 605 B.C. to 536 B.C.). We have purposely left out letters from the spelling of this month, as the name of this month is actually the name of a Babylonian deity.

As shown in an earlier chapter, we are commanded by YEHOVAH to never utter the names of other mighty ones but shockingly the Jewish calendar has one of its months named after a false elohim. Interestingly, T_m_uz is also the month when Israel worshipped the golden calf at the base of Mount Sinai—which is a sad parallel and testament to the sin nature of the flesh.

As the verse above states, there was weeping for this false deity during an annual period of forty days which had been set aside to commemorate T_m_uz's untimely death. This weeping was held at the house of YEHOVAH—the sacred Temple. The temple priests must have sanctioned this direct offense against YEHOVAH or they would not have allowed it to occur.

But there were even greater offenses against the name of YEHOVAH by the religious leaders of Israel:

> Then said he unto me, Hast thou seen *this*, O son of man? turn thee yet again, *and* thou shalt see greater abominations than these. And he brought me into the inner court of YEHOVAH's house, and, behold, at the door of the temple of YEHOVAH, between the porch and the altar, *were* about five and twenty men, with their backs toward the temple of YEHOVAH, and their

faces toward the east; and they worshipped the sun toward the east.

EZEKIEL 8:15-16

They worshipped the sun! The sun in this verse is not interpreted as a symbol for the Son of Elohim—there is nothing sacred about this reference. The religious leaders of the Temple took the sun worship teachings learned during their captivity in foreign lands and performed pagan abominations in the house of YEHOVAH.

There are other offences recorded in the original covenant that are not recounted here but are just as shocking to consider. It seems that YEHOVAH had enough of Israel's offenses when He proclaimed the following through the prophet Ezekiel:

> As for you, O house of Israel, thus saith YEHOVAH; Go ye, serve ye every one his idols, and hereafter *also*, if ye will not hearken unto me: **but pollute ye my holy name no more** with your gifts, and with your idols.
>
> EZEKIEL 20:39

YEHOVAH must have been hurt because He goes on to make a heartfelt admission:

> But I had pity for **mine holy name**, which the house of Israel had profaned among the heathen, whither they went.
>
> Ezekiel 36:21

This is such a saddening verse. The Creator of the whole universe opens His heart to His prophet to admit that He is sorrowful for how His children trod on His holy name. Imagine how you would feel if your children, whom you love, ignored you, or gave the credit for the gifts you had given to them to others, or had disdain and contempt for you. How can we, His creation, do this to YEHOVAH? Saved or not saved, under grace or not under grace, filled with the Holy Spirit or an unfilled vessel—regardless—YEHOVAH is still our Elohim!

Non-scriptural worship offends and pollutes the name of YEHOVAH. If we truly wish to worship YEHOVAH we must avoid polluting His holy name. It's our responsibility to keep the Name pure in our lives—that is, if we accept that YEHOVAH wants His name honored.

> In their setting of their threshold by my thresholds, and their post by my posts, and the wall between me and them, they have even defiled **my holy name** by their abomi-

nations that they have committed: wherefore I have consumed them in mine anger.

ZEKIEL 43:8

We have shown verses that demonstrate how the religious leaders in the past profaned the name (reputation) of YEHOVAH but what about the current religious leaders of Judaism and Christianity—have they done so as well?

In our opinion the answer is *yes*—the most critical offense is the hiding of the true pronunciation of the name of YEHOVAH by the current religious leaders. While they may argue that the true pronunciation of YEHOVAH was lost over time, do you really believe that something as precious as the true pronunciation of the name of the Creator of the whole universe, who desires and commands His name to be known across the whole world, was tossed aside like a worn-out shoe by those who were entrusted with it?

Throughout history the most powerful Christian denominations have contributed to this deception by their insistence on hiding the fact that our Creator actually has a real name by using the misleading title "the LORD" to address him. Could the root of this be from hidden anti-Semitism or perhaps from a conscious desire of the Church fathers to distance themselves and their followers from the Hebrew roots of the faith, or from the blinding power of the traditions of men?

But what about each of us, have we profaned YEHOVAH's name? If we have, even if unconsciously, we must strive to change our ways by eliminating the doctrines and traditions of men that are an *abomination* to Elohim. Why? Not because we have to, but because we love Him and want to please Him as best we can.

Does YEHOVAH care about His name? If you aren't convinced yet consider this next verse:

> Behold, I [YEHOVAH] have refined you [Israel], but not as silver; I have tested you in the furnace of affliction. For My own sake, for My own sake, I will act; For how can *My name* be profaned? And My glory I will not give to another.
> ISAIAH 48:10-11 (NAS)

In Isaiah Chapter 48, YEHOVAH recounts the insolence of Israel towards Him. In order to protect His name He puts them through hardships in an effort to purge them of unrighteousness. You who are parents know how painful it is to watch your children suffer during periods of punishment yet there are times when punishment is the only proper and loving way to instruct them for their own benefit.

The title of this chapter "Keeping the Name Pure" is somewhat of a misnomer as the name of YEHOVAH, in and of itself, is and will always be pure. Rather it is our hearts and our actions that must remain pure to the Name. Yet, within this fallen world the set-apart name has become of "none effect" by the failure of men to treat it with the honor and respect it deserves.

But how can we, who have inherited a sin nature from our fallen ancestors ever hope to live a righteous and holy life and do justice to the Name? The answer is by being born again in the Holy Spirit—the set-apart Spirit whose duty and privilege it is to fulfill the will of the Creator. When we are baptized in the Holy Spirit our spirit-man inside becomes pure (it is a brand new creation) and we are thus able to worship YEHOVAH in spirit and in truth for our spirit is then made identical to Yehoshua's:

> Herein is our love made perfect, that we may have boldness in the day of judgment: because as he [Yehoshua] is, so are we in **this** world.
> I JOHN 4:17

If you desire to know Elohim and deepen your personal relationship with His Son Yehoshua you need to be born again and baptized in the Holy Spirit—just

Proclaim His Holy Name

as those in the early church were. If you desire to understand the Word with deeper insight and connection you need to be born again and baptized in the Holy Spirit. And if you desire to honor the name of the Creator (as He desires), and to keep His name pure in your heart, you need to be born again and baptized in the Holy Spirit. For when you are, you will be as Yehoshua is, not only in the world to come, but also in your life on Earth right now.

Chapter 11

JERUSALEM—WHERE THE NAME HAS BEEN PLACED

> And he built altars in the house of YEHOVAH, of which YEHOVAH said, In Jerusalem will I put my **name**.
>
> II KINGS 21:4

Of all the cities in the world only one city was chosen by YEHOVAH as His city where His holy set-apart name would be placed forever. He did not choose to place His name in Rome nor did He choose to place His name in Mecca or Medina. YEHOVAH chose Jerusalem—the city on Earth which is closest to the mountain where Abraham was asked to sacrifice the son he loved, Isaac, as an offering to Elohim. That mountain, Mount Moriah, is the site of the first and second temples of YEHOVAH. And on that mountain, in Pilate's fortress, Elohim's son Yehoshua was sentenced to die so that through his sacrifice we might live and have eternal life.

The meaning of the name Jerusalem comes from two parts: "Jeru" which means *"to show"* or *"to teach"* and "Salem" which means *"peace"* or *"harmony."* Therefore "Jerusalem" can mean *"teaching of peace"* and *"show harmony."* However, it is traditionally called "The City of Peace" and its name is recorded over 750 times in the King James Bible.

To show how very important this city is to YEHOVAH consider the next verse from Isaiah. The special terms used to describe the city reinforce the complete personal connection that the Creator of ALL things has with Jerusalem and the promised land:

> Thou [Jerusalem] shalt no more be termed Forsaken; neither shall thy land any more be termed Desolate: but thou shalt be called Hephzibah, and thy land Beulah: for YEHOVAH delighteth in thee, and thy land shall be married.
>
> ISAIAH 62:4

The word "Hephzibah" means *"my delight is in her"* while the meaning of the word "Beulah" is *"bride."* YEHOVAH so loves Jerusalem and the land that He will make a covenant akin to marriage between them. And you can be sure that YEHOVAH will honor this covenant as He alone is good and righteous (Mark 10:18).

Even though Jerusalem is called the "City of Peace" it has been the site of many battles. It will also be the site of an epic battle in the "end times." In the book of Zechariah, chapters 12 through 14, Zechariah writes that YEHOVAH will defend Jerusalem and Judah against all attackers. He uses a term repeatedly: "in that day" or "on that day." What "day" is Zechariah referring to? It is the day that all people of the Earth are gathered against Jerusalem:

> And **in that day** will I make Jerusalem a burdensome stone for **all** people: **all** that burden themselves with it shall be cut in pieces, though **all the people of the earth** be gathered together against it.
>
> ZECHARIAH 12:3

In that day, Zechariah prophesied that YEHOVAH will do the following on behalf of Jerusalem and Israel:

• Strike every horse and rider coming against Jerusalem with confusion.	• Make the leaders of Israel like a flaming torch consuming all their enemies.
• Destroy *all* the nations that attack Jerusalem.	• Shield those who live in Jerusalem.
• Banish the *names* of the idols so they will be remembered no more.	• Pour out a spirit of grace upon the house of David and the inhabitants of Jerusalem.

• Remove the prophets and the spirit of impurity from the land—there shall no more be prophets in the land.	• Provide a fountain to the house of David and the inhabitants of Jerusalem to purge them from sin and impurity.
• When it is nighttime there will be light.	• Living waters will flow out from Jerusalem to both eastern and western seas.
• Stand on the Mount of Olives and split it in two from east to west.	• There will be only one Elohim over all the Earth whose name is YEHOVAH.

*Table references taken from Zechariah chapters 12-14

Even though the "end times" battles are destined to occur there is a well known verse in the book of Psalms that encourages us to pray for the peace of Jerusalem:

> Pray for the peace of Jerusalem: they shall prosper that love thee.
>
> PSALMS 122:6

When you pray for the peace of Jerusalem you are actually praying for the return of the Messiah because only after the events of "in that day" come to pass will there be true peace—Elohim's peace, rather than the peace of fallen man. In that day, Yehoshua will return as the conquering King, the long-awaited Messiah of the Jews, and he will rule with an iron rod:

> And out of his [Messiah's] mouth goeth a sharp sword, that with it he should smite the nations: and he shall rule them with a rod of iron: and he treadeth the winepress of the fierceness and wrath of El Shaddai.
> REVELATION 19:15

Jerusalem, the holy city, is a city set-apart from all other cities as it is not only where YEHOVAH has placed His name, but it is also where Yehoshua will rule and reign from for 1000 years:

> And I saw thrones, and they sat upon them, and judgment was given unto them: and *I saw* the souls of them that were beheaded for the witness of Yehoshua, and for the Word of Elohim, and which had not worshipped the beast, neither his image, neither had received *his* mark upon their foreheads, or in their hands; and **they lived and reigned with Messiah a thousand years**.
> REVELATION 20:4

Until the "end times" come to pass we can rely on the promises that YEHOVAH has made in His name regarding His holy city. These promises revolve around a special anointing that has been placed on the Holy Temple and Jerusalem. Consider the following prayer by King Solomon to YEHOVAH and YEHOVAH's response:

Solomon's Request

> If they return to thee with all their heart and with all their soul in the land of their captivity, whither they have carried them captives, and pray toward their land, which thou gavest unto their fathers, and *toward* the city which thou hast chosen, and toward the house which I have built for thy name: Then hear thou from the heavens, *even* from thy dwelling place, their prayer and their supplications, and maintain their cause, and forgive thy people which have sinned against thee.
> II CHRONICLES 6:38-39

YEHOVAH's Response

> If my people, which are called by my **name**, shall humble themselves, and pray, and seek my face, and turn from their wicked ways; then will I hear from heaven, and will

forgive their sin, and will heal their land.
>
> II CHRONICLES 7:14

Another promise in YEHOVAH's name about the city of Jerusalem is found in the book of Joel where the prophet states that whoever calls on the name of YEHOVAH will be saved. Note that he does not say whoever calls on the title "the LORD" will be saved. If you wish to be saved shouldn't you call on the *name* and not a *title?*

> And it shall come to pass, *that* whosoever shall **call on the name** of YEHOVAH shall be delivered: for in mount Zion and in Jerusalem shall be deliverance, as YEHOVAH hath said, and in the remnant whom YEHOVAH shall call.
>
> JOEL 2:32

To those of you who are Gentiles and who love the name of YEHOVAH a special blessing is promised you in His name regarding His holy mountain and His holy Temple:

> Also the sons of the stranger [Gentiles], that join themselves to YEHOVAH, to serve him, and to **love the name** of YEHOVAH,

> to be his servants, every one that keepeth the sabbath from polluting it, and taketh hold of my covenant; Even them will I bring to my holy mountain, and make them joyful in my house of prayer: their burnt offerings and their sacrifices *shall be* accepted upon mine altar; for mine house shall be called an house of prayer for all people.
>
> ISAIAH 56:6-7

Some of you may have already experienced this blessing. We have. After several years of planning we made our first trip to Israel in 2009 and experienced the sense of peace and belonging that exists there. We hope to return someday and spend more time in YEHOVAH's holy city Jerusalem. However, Jerusalem will not always be called by the name Jerusalem. At some point, most likely after the battle of the "end times," the Word makes it clear that Jerusalem itself will be called by a new *unknown* name:

> For Zion's sake will I [YEHOVAH] not hold my peace, and for Jerusalem's sake I will not rest, until the righteousness thereof go forth as brightness, and the salvation thereof as a lamp *that* burneth. And the Gentiles shall see thy [Jerusalem's] righteousness,

and all kings thy glory: and **thou shalt be called by a new name**, which the mouth of YEHOVAH shall name. Thou shalt also be a crown of glory in the hand of YEHOVAH, and a royal diadem in the hand of thy Elohim.

ISAIAH 62:1-3

Could that new name be what the prophet Jeremiah wrote of?

In those days shall Judah be saved, and Jerusalem shall dwell safely: and this *is the name* wherewith she shall be called, **YEHOVAH our righteousness**.

JEREMIAH 33:16

While we do not know for certain which new name YEHOVAH will choose for Jerusalem we can safely assume that whatever name He chooses will have an exact meaning that represents its new spirit. We know this because of the care that is shown throughout the scriptures regarding the naming of Biblical personalities and places. Even though we don't know the specific name, we do know from the Word that Jerusalem will be known as the "City of Truth."

> Thus saith YEHOVAH; I am returned unto Zion, and will dwell in the midst of Jerusalem: and Jerusalem shall be called a **city of truth**; and the mountain of YEHOVAH of hosts the holy mountain.
>
> ZECHARIAH 8:3

We also know from the Word that *all* nations will come to the mountain of Elohim for instruction and fellowship:

> And it shall come to pass in the last days, *that* the mountain of YEHOVAH's house shall be established in the top of the mountains, and shall be exalted above the hills; and all nations shall flow unto it. And many people shall go and say, Come ye, and let us go up to the mountain of YEHOVAH, to the house of the Elohim of Jacob; and he will teach us of his ways, and we will walk in his paths: for out of Zion shall go forth the law, and the word of YEHOVAH from Jerusalem.
>
> ISAIAH 2:2-3

The word "Torah" makes most Christians uncomfortable. "Torah" can mean direction or instruction yet most Christians consider it to mean the "Law" and are anti-Torah because of their misunderstanding of the writings of Paul regarding Grace and the Law. But if you consider the word *Torah* as *instruction*—instruction from Elohim on how to live a prosperous, blessed, and righteous life then any enmity that you hold in your heart for the Word (Torah) of YEHOVAH will dissolve.

Even though there is a new covenant that extends eternal life to those who believe in the name of Yehoshua, the original covenant is still in force as all has not yet been fulfilled. For the Messiah has said the following when speaking of the Torah:

> For verily I say unto you, Till **heaven and earth pass**, one jot or one tittle[1] shall in no wise pass from the law, till **all** be fulfilled. Whosoever therefore shall break one of these least commandments, and shall teach men so, he shall be called the least in the kingdom of heaven: but whosoever shall do and teach *them*, the same shall be called great in the kingdom of heaven.
> MATTHEW 5:18-19

The Spring feasts of YEHOVAH (Passover, Unleavened Bread, First Fruits, Pentecost) were shadow pictures pointing to the Messiah as the suffering servant and have already been fulfilled. But the Fall feasts of YEHOVAH (The Day of Trumpets, Atonement, Tabernacles) which revolve around the Messiah returning as the conquering King have not yet been fulfilled. This is why we say that *all* has not yet been fulfilled, i.e., the *position* of the conquering King will not be "*filled*" until the day that Yehoshua returns.

Therefore, since the Torah has not yet passed away and YEHOVAH's name has been placed in Jerusalem and on Mount Moriah, YEHOVAH still hears the prayers made towards the holy city and the temple mount. He states without doubt that His name will be there forever and His heart as well:

> But unto the place which YEHOVAH your Elohim shall choose out of all your tribes to put his name there, *even* unto his habitation shall ye seek, and thither thou shalt come:
> DEUTERONOMY 12:5

> And YEHOVAH said unto him, I have heard thy prayer and thy supplication, that thou hast made before me: I have hallowed this house, which thou hast built, to put **my name there for ever**; and mine eyes and

mine heart **shall be there perpetually**.

I KINGS 9:3

This is exactly the feeling one gets when standing at the Western wall at the base of the Temple Mount (also known as the *Wailing Wall*)—that YEHOVAH's hand is still there today and His power and divine Spirit continue to flow on Mount Moriah where His name resides forever. This is also where the "one-new-man," Jew and Gentile together will become a reality someday (Ephesians 2:14-15). When the "one-new-man" does come to pass which of the three possibilities below do you think it will manifest as?

    a. That the Jews will renounce the Torah and accept Yehoshua as Elohim?

    b. That the Christians will renounce Yehoshua as the Messiah and follow only the Torah?

    c. That Jews will accept Yehoshua as the prophesied Messiah and as their King, in the line of David AND the Christians will accept that the Jew is the ROOT and that they are connected to the ROOT as a VINE is connected to the ROOT by a BRANCH which is Yehoshua, the King of the Jews? (Jeremiah 23:5)

Many Christians believe the answer is option "a." They believe Yehoshua came to create a new religion in the Galilee called Christianity. Orthodox Jews would overwhelmingly choose option "b" as they do not believe Yehoshua is the true Messiah. Rather than "a" or "b" being correct, we believe that option "c" is correct because Yehoshua taught: *"I am the way, the truth, and the life: no man cometh unto the Father, but by me"* (John 14:6) and that *"salvation is of the Jews."*

> Yehoshua saith unto her, Woman, believe me, the hour cometh, when ye shall neither in this mountain, nor yet at Jerusalem, worship the Father. Ye worship ye know not what: we know what we worship: for **salvation is of the Jews**. But the hour cometh, and now is, when the true worshippers shall worship the Father in spirit and in truth: for the Father seeketh such to worship him. Elohim *is* a Spirit: and they that worship him must worship *him* in spirit and in truth.
>
> JOHN 4:21-24

While all of the promises and the wisdom of Elohim's Torah still apply today, and the Word of YEHOVAH proves the importance of Jerusalem and the Temple, the Messiah shows us a deeper layer of worship and honor that is tied to the Holy Spirit and to the Kingdom of Heaven that is at hand (*the hour cometh and now is*).

We used to believe that the phrase "The Kingdom of Heaven is at hand" meant that the "last days" are close and that the prophecies contained in the Fall Feasts were about to be made evident. However, the Messiah used this phrase 2000 years ago and the Fall Feast prophecies weren't fulfilled at that time. This is because the phrase "The Kingdom of Heaven is at hand" actually means that the will of YEHOVAH, His forgiveness, His desire to fellowship, and the power and truth of His Holy Spirit was available RIGHT THEN as Yehoshua preached.

Part of the GOOD NEWS of the Gospel is that the Kingdom of Heaven is at hand NOW. The power and the truth of the Holy Spirit has been available all believers since the day of Pentecost. It is up to each of us to ask for the Baptism of the Holy Spirit and to renew our hearts and minds in Messiah.

With the anointing of the Holy Spirit flowing in your life you can worship as Yehoshua prophesied, not only at the holy mountain where the temples have been built (and where all people will come to worship YEHOVAH someday) but also in the spirit within your temple, your being, wherever you are on Earth. Those born again in the Spirit have become a new creation and their spirit is perfected before YEHOVAH—ready for fellowship and the inheritance promised to a favored son.

> Him that overcometh will I [Yehoshua] make a pillar in the temple of my Elohim [YEHOVAH], and he shall go no more out: and I will write upon him the **name** of my Elohim, and the **name** of the city of my Elohim, *which is* new Jerusalem, which cometh down out of heaven from my Elohim: and *I will write upon him* my new **name**.
> REVELATION 3:12

Chapter 12

PURE PRAISE PURE WORSHIP

> Let them praise the name of YEHOVAH: for his name alone is excellent; his glory *is* above the earth and heaven.
>
> PSALMS 148:13

King David, the most famous king of ancient Israel, was also the greatest praise and worship leader of all time. He has been credited with writing the verse above as well as most of the book of Psalms—a book full of pure prayer, praise, and worship to Elohim.

David, the son of Jesse, was born in Bethlehem in the year 2892 from creation (1085 B.C.). His dramatic rise from shepherd boy to the throne of Israel is one of the most well known stories in the Bible. Yet it wasn't because of his great outward feats that David was chosen by YEHOVAH to be king of Israel but rather because of what lay inside his heart:

> But YEHOVAH said unto Samuel, Look

> not on his [one of David's brothers] countenance, or on the height of his stature; because I have refused him: for *YEHOVAH seeth* not as man seeth; for man looketh on the outward appearance, but YEHOVAH **looketh on the heart**.
>
> I SAMUEL 16:7

It has been said of David that he was "a man after Elohim's own heart." This means that David was a man who desired and sought for a deep and meaningful relationship with YEHOVAH and to know and follow His will.

In I Samuel chapter 13, the prophet Samuel foreshadows the rise of David. In the following verses Samuel admonishes King Saul, David's predecessor. Saul was chosen to be the first king of Israel, but unfortunately he fell from grace when he disobeyed YEHOVAH (I Samuel 13:8-11). Because of Saul's self-righteousness, his relationship with Elohim was damaged. Saul had lost the favor of El Shaddai:

> And Samuel said to Saul, Thou hast done foolishly: thou hast not kept the commandment of YEHOVAH thy Elohim, which he commanded thee: for now would YEHOVAH have established thy kingdom upon Israel

> for ever. But now thy kingdom shall not continue: YEHOVAH hath sought him **a man after his own heart**, and YEHOVAH hath commanded him *to be* captain over his people, because thou hast not kept *that* which YEHOVAH commanded thee.
> I SAMUEL 13:13-14

The intent of Saul's heart was revealed by his act of disobeying Elohim. If he refused to entertain the *thought* of disobeying and had not *acted* on it then the favor of Elohim would have most likely remained upon Saul and we may never have heard of the name of David, son of Jesse. Yet, like Adam and Eve, who succumbed to temptation, Saul made a decision that separated him and his seed from YEHOVAH's blessing.

In contrast to Saul, David, as a "man after YEHOVAH's own heart," pursued Elohim as a young man would court a young woman. He wooed Elohim with a pure heart through his words, his music, and his song:

> My mouth shall speak the praise of YEHOVAH: and let all flesh bless his holy **name** for ever and ever.
> PSALMS 145:21

A pure heart creates pure praise that in turn creates a bridge to the heavens, facilitating communication between man and Elohim. Yehoshua, David's descendant and heir to the throne of Israel, taught us that a pure heart gains us access to the Father:

> Blessed *are* the pure in heart: for they shall see Elohim.
>
> MATTHEW 5:8

Purity of heart, in the context of the verse above, means that the heart is not polluted by worldly concerns. While one's heart may be currently covered with the carnality of this world, it lies within them, a perfect creation of YEHOVAH since the day they were born again. But how can one create a pure heart if they are overwhelmed by the duties and cares of this world? The correct question is actually "how does one cultivate a pure heart?" The answer is by praising and worshipping YEHOVAH in spirit and in truth. Similar to a gardener who makes the soil rich by tilling, praise and worship helps prepare your heart for the seed of the Word to be planted within it. As the Word takes root in your heart it will grow into a tree that will bear good fruit. Let us praise YEHOVAH:

> Bless YEHOVAH, O my soul. O YEHOVAH

> my Elohim, thou art very great; thou art clothed with honour and majesty. Who coverest *thyself* with light as *with* a garment: who stretchest out the heavens like a curtain: Who layeth the beams of his chambers in the waters: who maketh the clouds his chariot: who walketh upon the wings of the wind: Who maketh his angels spirits; his ministers a flaming fire: *Who* laid the foundations of the earth, *that* it should not be removed for ever. Thou coveredst it with the deep as *with* a garment: the waters stood above the mountains.
>
> PSALMS 104:1-6

When you praise and worship Elohim you are to come before Him in childlike simplicity, raising your hands to Him who has created all, and opening your mouth to sing unto His name:

> Sing forth the honour of his name: make his praise glorious.
>
> PSALMS 66:2

Why is praise so important? Pure praise creates an environment for us to communicate with YEHOVAH and Yehoshua unfettered by the pull of the carnal self. Therefore pure praise is important because it creates a supernatural environment that opens a pipeline between the material and spiritual worlds. In this way praise is similar to prayer, for prayer is communication with Elohim. However, while prayer can deteriorate into a one-sided list of requests, pure praise never fails to lift up the name of YEHOVAH.

How much did David love YEHOVAH? The next verse from Psalm 45 shows both the level of David's love as well as YEHOVAH's desire for His name to be known to all people. How do we know this? Because of the promise that David makes to Elohim. If you were trying to woo someone would you promise them something that was of no value to them?

> I will make **thy name** to be remembered in all generations: therefore shall the people praise thee forever and ever.
>
> PSALMS 45:17

David's promise was to make Elohim's name remembered so the people would praise YEHOVAH forever. Thus we see, through David's eyes, what is valuable to Elohim. David clearly fulfilled this promise to YEHOVAH. If you are in doubt, pick up your Bible and take the time to read and meditate on each of the Psalms and you will come to no other conclusion.

Yet even though David fulfilled his promise to Elohim, the leaders of Judaism and Christianity (who claim David as a patriarch) have made David's efforts of "none effect" by not proclaiming the name of Elohim themselves. For how can YEHOVAH's name be remembered—by all people in all generations—if His name has not been revealed and declared? You can't be expected to remember something you were never taught!

When you begin to praise Elohim you must put aside your human needs and ignore the unending demands of the carnal mind. By doing so you will uncover your heart before Elohim. It will show Elohim that you trust Him with your life. YEHOVAH will honor that praise and *inhabit* it with His sacred presence:

> But thou *art* holy, O *thou* that inhabitest
> the praises of Israel.
> PSALMS 22:3

Choosing Your Words

When you are courting your beloved you choose your words with care. They are an outward manifestation of your heart. Therefore, the words that we choose to praise and worship YEHOVAH with must be paid attention to—not as some magical mantra but to ensure that they accurately communicate our intents towards Elohim.

For example, consider the following two statements from the point of view of the one you were trying to woo. Imagine how they would feel and respond to you if they heard the following words:

> 1). Beloved, I am so unworthy of you. In my desperation I implore you to be with me and to love me for without you I am of no value.

> 2). Beloved, your beauty is beyond compare. Your heart is gentle and kind and your love is like a sweet fragrance in the air.

Believe it or not the first statement above is typical of how most praise and worship music of today tries to honor and glorify Elohim. Webster defines praise as *"to express a favorable judgment of"* and *"to glorify especially by the attribution of perfection."* Choice #1 above does neither, rather it tells YEHOVAH that you do not trust that He is with you and that He loves you. It does not honor or glorify Elohim—therefore it is *not* praise.

And what of worship? The word "worship" is derived from the middle English word "worshipe" which means *"worthiness, respect, reverence paid to a divine being.*" Therefore worship is the act of acknowledging he who is worthy. Who among us is worthy and therefore deserving of worship? Our Elohim, the Father and Creator of all:

> And I John saw these things, and heard *them.* And when I had heard and seen, I fell down to worship before the feet of the angel which shewed me these things. Then saith he unto me, See *thou do it* not: for I am thy fellowservant, and of thy brethren the prophets, and of them which keep the sayings of this book: **worship Elohim**.
> REVELATION 22:8-9

In the passage above the angel of YEHOVAH admonishes John to worship Elohim and not the created beings as we are all servants of the Creator. As servants of YEHOVAH, and in agreement with the angel of Revelation, we are instructed by King David, once again, to praise Elohim's holy name:

> Praise ye YEHOVAH. Praise ye the name of YEHOVAH; praise *him*, O ye **servants** of YEHOVAH.
> PSALMS 135:1

Did you notice that the statement made earlier: *"Beloved, I am so unworthy of you. In my desperation I implore you to be with me and to love me for without you I am of no value"* focuses on the person trying to woo the other and not the object of affection—in other words it is self-centered? Do not mix your praise and worship with unbelief, weakness, or self-centeredness. This dilutes and pollutes your praise—your praise is no longer pure.

We refer to this diluted type of praise and worship as "sad-sack worship." Sad Sack was an old comic book character. He was a private in the Army who always looked for the easy way out. Basically he was just plain lazy. This is what a great deal of praise and worship music of today is like. We are begging Elohim to release His spirit, to bring revival, to heal us, to make us worthy when He has already provided all these things (John 4:14, 7:38). It is not Elohim who is blocking the blessings of born-again spirit-filled believers rather it is they who are blocking it by not understanding, accepting, and acting on the "believer's authority" (Mark 11:23-24).

You can avoid sad-sack worship by first identifying it. The next time that you attend a worship service *focus* on the words being sung. Are they mournful, sorrowful, or non-victorious? Do they glorify YEHOVAH for all He has given us? Are the words you are singing affirming life (not only in Heaven but here on Earth) or focusing on your own weaknesses? Are they allowing Elohim's power to flow in your life or shutting it down? If they are mournful, focus on defeat, or shut down the flow of spirit then it can be classified as sad-sack worship.

Now that you are able to identify sad-sack worship, the next step is to reject that form of worship. Do *not* sing those words for the Bible says that death and life are in the power of the tongue (Proverbs 18:21).

The final step in recognizing and eliminating sad-sack worship is to declare the great and holy name of Elohim with joy and thanksgiving—looking for NOTHING in return—for our worship should be a sign of our love and desire for relationship with Elohim and for no other purpose:

> Enter into his gates with thanksgiving, *and* into his courts with praise: be thankful unto him, *and* bless his name.
>
> PSALMS 100:4

David, our praise and worship leader, teaches us that praise is giving credit to YEHOVAH for all He has done and that we are to show our commitment to our relationship with Elohim by entering into His holy presence with an offering:

> Give unto YEHOVAH the glory *due unto* his name: **bring an offering**, and come into his courts.
>
> PSALMS 96:8

YEHOVAH, the King of the entire universe, is faithful and just—He has given us the gift of life and everything we need to prosper here on Earth. Even though we praise and worship with no thought of return, Elohim knows our every need and is good to us (Matthew 7:11). Like a good father, He will not give us a stone instead of a fish nor a scorpion instead of an egg (Luke 11:12), neither will He be like the *unjust* judge who eventually gave in to the incessant demands of the widow (Luke 18:1-6). We need not badger Him like the widow badgered the unjust judge because our Elohim brings justice swiftly and without delay for He is righteous. Elohim has clothed us like the lilies of the field. We do not need to beg. Even if we "knock" on Elohim's door at midnight He will not turn us away (Luke 11:5-10). YEHOVAH has given us gifts of whose value we cannot comprehend with our carnal mind including the gift of salvation:

> Sing unto YEHOVAH, bless his name; shew forth his salvation from day to day.
>
> PSALMS 96:2

Pure Praise Pure Worship

In Psalms 96:2 David tells us that we should bless YEHOVAH's name through singing. Yet sadly, almost all of contemporary praise and worship music is devoid of Elohim's name. They may sing *of* the name but they do not lift up His name. Why? Because they do not *use* His holy name.

Consider how many worship songs use the term "Lord" and the name of the pagan deity "G_d." As you have been taught, Elohim's name is not "the LORD" nor "G_d," so as you praise and worship Him use His *name*, not the word "name" nor the incorrect name "Lord" or "G_d" but His name יהוה (Yah or Yehovah). We urge you to sing out the true name of Elohim whenever you see the false names.

For example in the song "How Great is Our G_d" we are told that the Name is above all other names and that our "G_d" is great, but we are never asked to sing His actual name! The same is true in the song "Blessed be Your Name." In it we are asked to sing over and over again that the name of the Lord is blessed, however not once do we sing His actual name. Both of these songs could easily be sung by people of other religions who do not worship Yehoshua's Father YEHOVAH (the Elohim of Abraham, Isaac, and Jacob).

Also note that there is a good example of sad-sack worship in "Blessed be Your Name." The lyrics state that the Father is someone who *takes away* from us. This is not correct. It is not YEHOVAH but rather Satan who is the destroyer (John 10:10). The lyrics contain a depressing message that is not the Gospel of Yehoshua—for Yehoshua, who did only the will of the Father, healed all who came to him. YEHOVAH doesn't send disease to take away life but rather gives both life and His Spirit to those who love Him and His holy name.

YEHOVAH is a good Elohim. If you don't believe us then read the words of Messiah Yehoshua:

> If ye then, being evil, know how to give good gifts unto your children, how much more shall your Father [YEHOVAH] which is in heaven give good things to them that ask him?"
>
> MATTHEW 7:11

Some of you may think that we are being too critical, however we are not condemning the writers of the songs, but rather we are questioning the song lyrics themselves. Once you know that YEHOVAH wants His name to be used and known, why would you resist honoring that? Consider what Stephen, the first martyr, proclaimed to the religious leaders as they persecuted him for preaching in the name of Yehoshua:

> Ye stiffnecked and uncircumcised in heart and ears, ye do always resist the Holy Ghost: as your fathers *did*, so *do* ye.
> ACTS 7:51

Stephen was quoting Elohim who used the term "stiffnecked" people several times in referring to the rebellious and self-righteous among the children of Israel. And what is self-righteousness? It is enmity for YEHOVAH's Torah. It is saying to Elohim, in essence, "I don't need You, or Your input. My law supersedes Your law."

> And YEHOVAH said unto Moses, I have seen this people, and, behold, it *is* a stiffnecked people:
> EXODUS 32:9

Now that you've learned a better way to praise Elohim, consider *when* you should praise Him. Certainly you should praise Him on Shabbat, at your church or temple—this we can see from David's declaration below:

> A Psalm *or* Song for the sabbath day. *It is a* good *thing* to give thanks unto YEHOVAH,

and to sing praises unto thy name, O most High:

>   PSALMS 92:1

I will declare thy **name** unto my brethren: in the midst of the congregation will I praise thee.

>   PSALMS 22:22

Yet David tells us to praise Elohim not only during formal religious services at our churches and temples—he instructs us to praise Elohim's name all day long:

From the rising of the sun unto the going down of the same YEHOVAH's **name** *is* to be praised.

>   PSALMS 113:3

This means we should praise YEHOVAH all day long; at home, at school, and at our place of work. No matter where we are or who we are with, or whether it is politically correct, or if others will not like us if we do—we are to praise His holy name.

When you don't feel like praising you should simply ignore your mind and emotions and praise Him anyway because praising Elohim will fill you with the glory of His presence.

Praise strengthens you against the temptations of Satan (Psalms 8:1-2). It will also give you the ability to fulfill your destiny just as it did for King David, ruler of all Israel, as he proclaims in the following verse:

> So will I sing praise unto thy **name** for ever,
> that I may **daily perform my vows**.
> PSALMS 61:8

We hope that the information we've included in this chapter will stimulate you to go beyond the "traditions of men" and deepen your relationship with YEHOVAH. Don't forget to question the words being spoken over you during the praise and worship services at your church. Be bold and speak out to your pastors and worship leaders about the tone and message of the songs selected for praise and worship. Tell them you want to glorify the name of Elohim by actually singing His name! And if they don't agree, sing out YEHOVAH's name anyway. *If you don't the stones will* (Luke 19:40).

> Surely the righteous shall give thanks unto thy name: the upright shall dwell in thy presence.
> PSALMS 140:13

Proclaim His Holy Name

Chapter 13

THE CREATOR'S WILL

> Thou shalt not take the name of YEHOVAH thy Elohim in vain: for YEHOVAH will not hold *him* guiltless that taketh his name in vain.
>
> DEUTERONOMY 5:11

The common understanding of the phrase "taking the name in vain" is when a person uses the word G_d and combines it with a word such as "damn." However this is not an accurate interpretation. While taking the actual name YEHOVAH and mixing it with the profane in speech or writing is certainly wrong, virtually no one takes His actual name in *vain* in that manner.

Deuteronomy 5:11's often misunderstood command from the Creator of the whole universe holds a hidden clue to His will regarding His holy name. To uncover this clue we will review the meaning of two words from the verse above, "vain" and "guiltless."

Strong's concordance states that the Hebrew word לשׁוא (transliterated as la·sha·ve), and traditionally translated to English as "vain" comes from the Hebrew root word שׁוא (transliterated as shav). Shav means *"emptiness"* or *"vanity."* It is translated in the English Bible as several different words: deceit, deceitful, deception, emptiness, empty, false, false visions, falsehood, lies, vain, vanity, and worthless.

Webster defines "emptiness" as *"lacking reality, substance, meaning, value"* as in "hollow" as well as *"destitute of effect or force"* as in "an empty threat." It is also defined as *"having no purpose or result."* The word "vain" is defined as *"having no real value"* as in "vain pretensions" as well as *"marked by futility or ineffectualness"* as in "vain efforts to escape." "Vain" is also defined as *"having or showing undue or excessive pride in one's appearance or achievements."* However this last definition is unlikely to be the meaning used in Deuteronomy 5:11 given its context.

Consider the following alternative translation in light of the meanings of the words "emptiness" and "vain."

> Thou shalt not take the name of YEHOVAH thy Elohim **to none effect**: for YEHOVAH will not hold *him* guiltless that taketh his

name **to none effect**.

DEUTERONOMY 5:11

This translation is actually commanding us to not allow the name of YEHOVAH to come to emptiness as in "destitute of effect," "hollow," "having no result," and it is also commanding us to not allow the name of YEHOVAH to be used in a vain manner, i.e., in a "futile" or "ineffectual" way. All of which equate to *"none effect."*

The phrase "to none effect" used here is similar to the phrase Yehoshua used to admonish the Pharisees, who by their traditions, made the Word of Elohim of *"none effect"* (see Mark 7:13).

By changing the name of the Creator within the Bible to "the LORD" man has hidden YEHOVAH's name and made it of *"none effect!"* Our religious leaders claim to honor the Name but how can they since they don't use it and instead use the term "Lord" (Ba_l)? Since our religious leaders do not promote the true name, the followers are not led to give it the honor and glory it is due:

> How long shall *this* be in the heart of the prophets that prophesy lies? yea, *they are* prophets of the deceit of their own heart; Which think to cause my people to **forget**

> **my name** by their dreams which they tell every man to his neighbour, as their fathers **have forgotten my name** for Baal.
>
> Jeremiah 23:26-27

Before you say that the verse above is speaking only of the prophets, and not the pastors and ministers who overwhelmingly fail to proclaim the name YEHOVAH, consider the following verses:

> For the pastors are become brutish, and have not sought YEHOVAH: therefore they shall not prosper, and all their flocks shall be scattered.
>
> Jeremiah 10:21

> For both prophet and priest are profane; yea, in my house have I found their wickedness, saith YEHOVAH.
>
> Jeremiah 23:11

Those of you who are rabbis, pastors, reverends, priests, ministers, and evangelists—of you does YEHOVAH expect *all* of your words to glorify Him and no other elohim. He expects you to not allow His name to become of *"none effect!"* The sheep in your flock trust you, the shepherd caring for Messiah's sheep, and they follow in innocence:

> and whoever may cause to stumble one of the little ones believing in me [Yehoshua], better is it for him if a millstone is hanged about his neck, and he hath been cast into the sea.
> MARK 9:42 (YLT)

For those of you who are the sheep, listen closely for the voice of the true shepherd. If your pastor is not teaching the Word, or is teaching unbelief in the Word (e.g., regarding healing or salvation) then find a shepherd that is following the true shepherd Yehoshua. If you choose to follow those who come clothed in error or falsehood you are being led by the devious or the blind—either way you may end up in the wilderness where he (Satan) is searching for those he can devour (I Peter 5:8).

Take these words to heart for YEHOVAH will not hold guiltless those that disobey His Word, especially those who should know better—His priests. And what does the word "guiltless" mean? Webster defines guiltless simply as *"innocent."* The word "innocent" is defined as *"free from guilt or sin especially through lack of knowledge of evil"* and *"harmless in effect or intention."*

The fact that you now know of the command in Deuteronomy 5:11 *"Thou shalt not take the name of YEHOVAH thy Elohim to none effect: for YEHOVAH will not hold him guiltless that taketh his name to none effect"* (in case you had not before) means that your innocence for breaking this command cannot be supported any longer by a lack of knowledge—but you can still be found guiltless for past offenses and all your sin if you repent (turn away from that sin) and accept the salvation offered all people by YEHOVAH—the blood sacrifice of His only Begotten Son Yehoshua our Messiah. Praise His holy name!

We believe that most believers today do not intentionally desire to have the name of the Father come to *"none effect."* Those who desire to profane His name would probably not even be reading this book unless they had come to repentance. But since you now know what YEHOVAH expects, we urge you to meditate on Deuteronomy 5:11 and begin to give His name the honor it is due by *using* His name to great effect!

Yehoshua followed the Father's example when he explained to his disciples that those who had heard him speak, especially the religious leaders in the Temple, could no longer claim ignorance as proof of their innocence. The following verse makes this clear:

> If I had not come and spoken unto them,

they had not had sin: but now they have no cloak for their sin.

JOHN 15:22

For those of you who say you are not under the Law and that Yehoshua is your advocate before YEHOVAH we agree—YEHOVAH will accept whomever Yehoshua confesses before the Father (Matthew 10:32). However, who will be your advocate before Yehoshua? In other words, do you have a *personal* relationship with the Messiah? Having a personal relationship with Yehoshua is not knowing *of* him, rather it is *knowing* him.

It may seem arrogant to say that we can know the will of the Creator of all things but it is true—we can know His will. How can we know it? We can know what the Creator's will is by His Word—the written Word and the Word that came down from Heaven in the person of Messiah Yehoshua. We can also know His will through the Comforter, the Holy Spirit, that was sent in Yehoshua's name to show us *all* things.

First and foremost the will of YEHOVAH is for us to follow His instructions. If Adam and Eve had followed YEHOVAH's instructions in the Garden of Eden the whole human experience would have been very much different. Therefore by comparison we can assume that if we fail to follow the instructions of our

Elohim, regardless of our "saved" status, we can be creating unwelcome results in our lives.

In the following verse YEHOVAH makes it clear that we are to follow His instructions. He does this by using His name to reinforce His authority:

> My judgments ye do, and My statutes ye keep, to walk in them; I am YEHOVAH your Elohim;
>
> LEVITICUS 18:4 (YLT)

In Chapter 18 of Leviticus YEHOVAH tells Moses to speak a series of instructions to the children of Israel in YEHOVAH's name. They include:

- Do not follow the practices of the Egyptians
- Do not follow the practices of the Canaanites
- Obey the instructions of YEHOVAH
- Do not have incestuous relations
- Do not have adulterous relations
- Do not sacrifice their children to Mole_h
- Do not have homosexual relations
- Do not have sexual relations with animals

Before you state that these instructions are only

The Creator's Will

for the Israelites, YEHOVAH ends the chapter by making it clear that the instructions are not only for the children of Jacob:

> Ye shall therefore keep my statutes and my judgments, and shall not commit *any* of these abominations; *neither* any of your own nation, **nor any stranger** that sojourneth among you:
> LEVITICUS 18:26

In Chapter 19 of Leviticus YEHOVAH continues to instruct the people on how they should behave lest the land spew them out as it did those that came before them. Fifteen times in this chapter, YEHOVAH reinforces each instruction by making sure that the people know that they are *His* instructions. He does this not by saying "I am the LORD" but by using His personal name—adding the phrase "I am YEHOVAH" or "I am YEHOVAH your Elohim" to each instruction.

Did YEHOVAH give all these instructions to simply control the people? No. If you trust the Creator, as a child trusts a parent, then you will follow His instructions because you believe that they are in your best interest. Consider the list above from Leviticus 18—which instructions do you believe (in your heart) are not in your best interest?

You may also believe that the instructions in Leviticus 18 apply only to the land of Israel. Once again, even if they did, the *pattern* of YEHOVAH's ideal is shown in His instructions. Why would a nation want to go against the ideals of its Creator? If nations ignore the Creator and continue condoning (and in some cases protecting) actions that go against the divine law then the following could eventually happen to that nation:

> (For all these abominations have the men of the land done, which *were* before you, and the land is defiled); That the land spue not you out also, when ye defile it, as it spued out the nations that *were* before you.
> LEVITICUS 18:27-28

If the current nations of the Earth defile their own land, as the Canaanites once did to theirs, then to where will the inhabitants of those nations be "spued?"

> The Son of man [Yehoshua] shall send forth his angels, and they shall gather out of his kingdom all things that offend, and them which do iniquity; And shall cast them into a furnace of fire: there shall be wailing and

gnashing of teeth.

MATTHEW 13:41-42

Similar to the Creator's will as found in the Torah, YEHOVAH has made His will regarding His holy name abundantly clear in other books of the Bible. The following verses show that YEHOVAH wants His name to be known to all and not hidden away in the dark:

<u>The Gentiles Shall Know His Name</u>
> So will I make **my holy name** known in the midst of my people Israel; and I will not *let them* pollute my holy name any more: **and the heathen shall know** that I *am* YEHOVAH, the Holy One in Israel.
>
> EZEKIEL 39:7

<u>They Shall Respect His Name</u>
> So shall they **fear* the name** of YEHOVAH from the west, and his glory from the rising of the sun. When the enemy shall come in like a flood, the Spirit of YEHOVAH shall lift up a standard against him.
>
> ISAIAH 59:19

* fear: *have profound adoring awed respect for*

The Name Shall Not be Polluted

But I [YEHOVAH] wrought for **my name's sake**, that it should not be polluted before the heathen, among whom they *were*, in whose sight I made myself known unto them, in bringing them forth out of the land of Egypt.

EZEKIEL 20:9

The Children Of Israel Shall Know His Name

Therefore, behold, I will this once cause them to know, I will cause them to know mine hand and my might; **and they shall know that my name *is* YEHOVAH**.

JEREMIAH 16:21

For His Holy Name's Sake

Therefore say unto the house of Israel, thus saith Adonai YEHOVAH; I do not *this* for your sakes, O house of Israel, but for **mine holy name's sake**, which ye have profaned among the heathen, whither ye went.

EZEKIEL 36:22

The Bible also teaches us YEHOVAH's will for His name by associating special attributes to the Name. The following chart shows various attributes of

YEHOVAH that reveal His will towards us—His desire for those who love Him. Note that some people believe the following phrases *are* the Father's name and they teach that YEHOVAH has many names. The Creator has one name and that is YEHOVAH (YHVH, see Ex. 3:15). Nevertheless, the Name when shown with the attributes below gives us confidence to know the Father's will, provision, and blessings for us:

Name/Attribute	Meaning	Verse
YEHOVAH-Yireh	YEHOVAH is our provider	Gn 22:14
YEHOVAH-Nissi	YEHOVAH is our banner	Ex 17:15
YEHOVAH-Rapha	YEHOVAH is our healer	Ex 15:26
YEHOVAH-Roi	YEHOVAH is our shepherd	Ps 23:1
YEHOVAH-Sabaoth	YEHOVAH is our protector	Ps 46:7
YEHOVAH-Shalom	YEHOVAH is our peace	Jgs 6:24
YEHOVAH-Tsidkenu	YEHOVAH is our righteousness	Jer 23:6

The Living Word

The written Word is clear about the importance of proclaiming the name of YEHOVAH to the world but what of the living Word—Yehoshua, the Son of the living Elohim? What can we learn about the will of the Creator through Yehoshua's words and actions?

First you must consider that Yehoshua did only what the Father did. This is seen in the following verse:

> Then answered Yehoshua and said unto them, Verily, verily, I say unto you, The Son can do nothing of himself, but what he seeth the Father do: for what things soever He doeth, these also doeth the Son likewise.
> JOHN 5:19

The Son has done nothing of himself. He has only done what the Father has done. Thus we can be assured that Yehoshua's words and actions not only support the will of the Father, but more importantly they make MANIFEST the will of the Father on Earth. Just as YEHOVAH proclaimed His own name to the whole world, the Messiah proclaimed the name of YEHOVAH to his disciples:

> I have **manifested thy name** unto the men which thou gavest me out of the world: thine they were, and thou gavest them me; and they have kept thy word.
> JOHN 17:6

The word "manifested" from John 17:6 is translated from the Greek word φανερόω (pronounced phaneroó). Phaneroó means *"to make visible or make clear."* Some English bibles translate the word "phaneroó" in a more modern way:

> I made **your name known** to the people you gave me. They are from this world. They belonged to you, and you gave them to me. They did what you told them.
> JOHN 17:6 (GWT)

Yehoshua taught us that no one lights a candle and places it under a basket where it is of no use but rather places it where it can shine and light one's way. Similarly no one who knows the Father name should hide the Name by replacing it with a title or feel that they should not speak it because religious leaders say that it is too holy to utter.

During his earthly ministry Yehoshua did not hide the light of the Father, nor the glory of the Father's Name. He fulfilled his Father's desire to make YEHOVAH's name known to all people. Who are we to do anything less? As Yehoshua did what he had seen the Father do, we should do what we have seen the Messiah do (as shown through the Word).

When Yehoshua entered into the city of Jerusalem before Passover (on the week he was to be sacrificed) a large crowd greeted him in the name of

YEHOVAH:

> And the multitudes that went before, and that followed, cried, saying, Hosanna to the son of David: Blessed *is* he that cometh **in the name of the Lord**; Hosanna in the highest.
>
> MATTHEW 21:9

Did the people really call out the name of a pagan deity "Ba_l" (Lord) instead of the name YEHOVAH when crying out to Yehoshua? To answer this we will consider a statement that the Messiah makes later after he had entered Jerusalem:

> O Jerusalem, Jerusalem, *thou* that killest the prophets, and stonest them which are sent unto thee, how often would I have gathered thy children together, even as a hen gathereth her chickens under *her* wings, and ye would not! Behold, your house is left unto you desolate. For I say unto you, Ye shall not see me henceforth, till ye shall say, Blessed *is* he that cometh in **the name of the Lord**.
>
> MATTHEW 23:37-39

Do you think Yehoshua was telling them "Blessed is he that comes in the name of Ba_l?" Of course not. Yehoshua was referring to the Father and was quoting from Psalms 118:26:

> Blessed *be* he that cometh in the name of YEHOVAH: we have blessed you out of the house of YEHOVAH.
>
> PSALMS 118:26

Based on Yehoshua's quote of Psalms 118:26 it is far more likely that the multitude in Matthew 21:9 were shouting:

> And the multitudes that went before, and that followed, cried, saying, Hosanna to the son of David: Blessed *is* he that cometh **in the name of YEHOVAH**; Hosanna in the highest.
>
> MATTHEW 21:9

When the religious leaders ordered Yehoshua to stop the crowd from crying out, he did not respond by rebuking the people but rather he told the priests that if the crowd stopped then the stones themselves would begin to shout—shout out the name of YEHOVAH! If the stones could shout it out, then we (who are greater than stones) should too.

The last command that the Messiah gave to his disciples (as recorded in the final two verses of the Gospel of Matthew) focuses on the Name:

> Go ye therefore, and teach all nations, baptizing them in the **name** of the Father, and of the Son, and of the Holy Ghost: Teaching them to observe all things whatsoever I have commanded you: and, lo, I am with you alway, *even* unto the end of the world. Amen.
>
> MATTHEW 28:19-20

This verse could be written as:

> Go ye therefore, and teach all nations, baptizing them in the name of **YEHOVAH**, and of **Yehoshua**, and of the **Ruach HaKodesh** [Holy Ghost in Hebrew]: Teaching them to observe all things whatsoever I have commanded you: and, lo, I am with you alway, *even* unto the end of the world. Amen.
>
> MATTHEW 28:19-20

Yehoshua did only what the Father did therefore Yehoshua's instructions are actually the Torah of the Father. And just as Yehoshua proclaimed that he would be with us always we can extrapolate that the Father is always with us as well. They are one. Let us forever honor the Creator's will by obeying the commandments of the Father and the Son—including the command to "not take the name of YEHOVAH in vain."

Proclaim His Holy Name

Chapter 14

CALLING ON THE NAME

> And to Seth, to him also there was born a son; and he called his name Enos: then began men to call upon the name of YEHOVAH.
>
> GENESIS 4:26

We call upon the Creator in our prayers—reaching out to Him at night before sleep or during times of personal or national crisis. Although most of us today don't call on Him using His name (since we aren't taught it), Biblical personalities of the past certainly did. According to Genesis 4:26, calling on the name of YEHOVAH goes back thousands of years to Adam's son Seth and his grandson Enos.

Seth was born when Adam was 130 years old and scripture tells us that Enos was born when Seth was 105 years old. This means that man began to call on the Creator by the name YEHOVAH in the year of creation 235. Before that we have no clear record of any name that may have been used by man to address Elohim.

Did Elohim respond to man's call? The Bible records only three men in between Adam and Abraham to whom YEHOVAH spoke directly: Cain—born sometime in the first century of creation, Enoch—born in the year 622 from creation, and Noah—born in the year 1056 from creation. While it is very possible that YEHOVAH spoke to more, such as Abel, we cannot tell this from the Word. It is more likely that after the murder of Abel by his brother Cain mankind's sin began to create barriers between themselves and the Creator:

> And YEHOVAH said unto Cain, Where *is* Abel thy brother? And he said, I know not: *Am* I my brother's keeper? And he said, What hast thou done? the voice of thy brother's blood crieth unto me from the ground. And now *art* thou cursed from the earth, which hath opened her mouth to receive thy brother's blood from thy hand;
> GENESIS 4:9-11

The next man after Cain who spoke directly with YEHOVAH was Enoch. Although the Word doesn't state this explicitly it does state that *"And Enoch walked with Elohim: and he was not; for Elohim took him"* (Genesis 5:24). This means that Enoch had found favor with YEHOVAH. In fact, he was so favored that he was translated into Heaven without ever having to die. From the time that Enoch was taken to Heaven in approximately the year 987 from creation until about the year 1556 from creation there is no mention of anyone calling on the name YEHOVAH nor YEHOVAH speaking to any other man—until Noah. The Word states that all mankind except for Noah (and a handful of his family members) had become wicked and every imagination of their heart was evil:

> And Elohim saw that the wickedness of man *was* great in the earth, and *that* every imagination of the thoughts of his heart *was* only evil continually. And it repented YEHOVAH that he had made man on the earth, and it grieved him at his heart.
> GENESIS 6:5-6

This rampant evil which included the mating of fallen angels with "the daughters of men" on the Earth (Genesis 6:4) resulted in Elohim making a momentous decision. YEHOVAH decided to send a great flood to destroy the evil that had covered the land:

> And Elohim said unto Noah, The end of

> all flesh is come before me; for the earth is filled with violence through them; and, behold, I will destroy them with the earth.
>
> GENESIS 6:13

After the great flood had purged evil from the Earth, the Word shows us that the great name of YEHOVAH was not lost for Noah himself proclaimed it:

> And he [Noah] said, Blessed *be* YEHOVAH Elohim of Shem; and Canaan shall be his servant.
>
> GENESIS 9:26

Noah lived another 350 years after the flood placing his death at approximately the year 2006 from creation. However, it was in the year 1948 from creation that the next man to whom YEHOVAH would speak directly with—Abraham—was born. It's interesting to note that it was in the year 1948 from Messiah's birth that the resurrected nation of Israel was reborn.

Abraham (Abram) was about 58 years old at the time of Noah's death. It was twelve years later that YEHOVAH began to speak directly to him. During the encounter documented in Genesis 12:1-3 we see the first Biblical reference to the famous covenant that YEHOVAH made with Abram:

Now YEHOVAH had said unto Abram, Get thee out of thy country, and from thy kindred, and from thy father's house, unto a land that I will shew thee: And I will make of thee a great nation, and I will bless thee, and make thy name great; and thou shalt be a blessing: And I will bless them that bless thee, and curse him that curseth thee: and in thee shall all families of the earth be blessed.

GENESIS 12:1-3

Abram obeyed YEHOVAH's instructions and left the land of his upbringing, taking with him his half sister Sarai (who was also his wife), his nephew Lot, and all their households. They journeyed to where YEHOVAH would lead them. At one point during the journey YEHOVAH reiterated the special promise He had made to Abram. Abram responded by building an altar and calling on the name of Elohim. It appears that Abram built the altar to serve as a visible marker or reminder of YEHOVAH's promise:

And YEHOVAH appeared unto Abram, and said, Unto thy seed will I give this land: and there builded he an altar unto YEHOVAH,

> who appeared unto him. And he removed from thence unto a mountain on the east of Bethel, and pitched his tent, *having* Bethel on the west, and Hai on the east: and there he built an altar unto YEHOVAH, and **called upon the name** of YEHOVAH.
>
> GENESIS 12:7-8

Abram, guided by Elohim, continued his travels but due to a famine in the land his plans were interrupted. Rather than continue their journey to the promised land, Abram and all his people went down into Egypt to find food. Later, after being expelled from Egypt because he withheld from Pharaoh the fact that Sarai was not only his sister but also his wife, Abram and the rest of his caravan traveled back to the area where YEHOVAH's original promises were made to him. Once there, Abram again called on the name of Elohim. Perhaps this was to reinforce the covenant YEHOVAH had made with him earlier at the site of the altar:

> Unto the place of the altar, which he had made there at the first: and there Abram **called on the name** of YEHOVAH.
>
> GENESIS 13:4

Years later, when Abram was ninety-nine years old, YEHOVAH once again reiterated His covenant with Abram as shown in the following verses:

> And when Abram was ninety years old and nine, YEHOVAH appeared to Abram, and said unto him, I *am* El Shaddai; walk before me, and be thou perfect. And I will make my covenant between me and thee, and will multiply thee exceedingly. And Abram fell on his face: and Elohim talked with him, saying, As for me, behold, my covenant *is* with thee, and thou shalt be a father of many nations. Neither shall thy name any more be called Abram, but thy name shall be Abraham; for a father of many nations have I made thee.
>
> GENESIS 17:1-5

The next scripture reference where Abraham called on the name of Elohim was when he made a covenant with Abimelech, the King of Gerar. The covenant secured back to Abraham ownership of a well he had originally dug that had been taken by Abimelech. This time, instead of building an altar to commemorate the covenant, Abraham planted a grove:

> Thus they made a covenant at Beersheba: then Abimelech rose up, and Phichol the chief captain of his host, and they returned into the land of the Philistines. And *Abraham* planted a grove in Beersheba, and **called there on the name** of YEHOVAH, the everlasting Elohim.
>
> GENESIS 21:32-33

YEHOVAH will provide

The series of promises YEHOVAH made to Abraham about his future offspring were brought to a climactic conclusion on the top of Mount Moriah in the year 2084 from creation. An angel of Elohim had just stopped Abraham from carrying out YEHOVAH's request that Abraham sacrifice the son he loved, Isaac, as a burnt offering. Abraham called the place that his son was spared *"YEHOVAH will provide"* because YEHOVAH Himself had provided a ram (the substitute for Isaac) for the sacrifice. This foreshadows how YEHOVAH would provide His own son Yehoshua as the final sacrifice for the redemption of mankind:

> And Abraham **called the name** of that place YEHOVAH-Jireh: as it is said *to* this day, In the mount of YEHOVAH it shall be seen.

> And the angel of YEHOVAH called unto Abraham out of heaven the second time, And said, By myself have I sworn, saith YEHOVAH, for because thou hast done this thing, and hast not withheld thy son, thine only *son*: That in blessing I will bless thee, and in multiplying I will multiply thy seed as the stars of the heaven, and as the sand which *is* upon the sea shore; and thy seed shall possess the gate of his enemies;
>
> GENESIS 22:14-17

Isaac, the beloved son of Abraham, later followed his father's example of building memorials and calling on the name of YEHOVAH when he himself received a promise from Elohim:

> And YEHOVAH appeared unto him [Isaac] the same night, and said, I *am* the Elohim of Abraham thy father: fear not, for I *am* with thee, and will bless thee, and multiply thy seed for my servant Abraham's sake. And he builded an altar there, and **called upon the name** of YEHOVAH, and pitched his tent there: and there Isaac's servants digged a well.
>
> GENESIS 26: 24-25

Just as the Bible patriarchs Abraham and Isaac created memorials to commemorate the promises they received from YEHOVAH, you too can create memorials to commemorate the promises you've received from YEHOVAH, Yehoshua, and the Holy Spirit.

The physical reminders you create can be as simple as writing down a list of the ways YEHOVAH has blessed you and then framing it, or any number of things as Spirit leads you. While the physical reminders will help you to focus on the promises of Elohim (like a mezuzah helps one remember the commands of YEHOVAH as they enter and leave their home) we suggest that you take the concept of creating memorials to a deeper level. Just as Yehoshua took the Torah to a deeper level by focusing on the actions of the heart rather than just the body, take the concept of erecting a physical reminder to a deeper level and build an altar in the temple of your heart—for it is there that you can worship YEHOVAH in Spirit and in Truth.

Elijah calls on the Name

We can choose to continue to call on "the LORD" (if we prefer to reach out to the Creator with a title derived from the name of a false elohim, i.e., Ba_l) but that is not what the prophet Elijah did when faced with certain death. In fact Elijah went up against the

450 prophets of Ba_l to demonstrate the greatness of YEHOVAH to the nation of Israel who had been led astray by the corrupt rulers King Ahab and his wife Jezebel.

King Ahab of Israel is recorded in the Bible as one of the worst transgressors of YEHOVAH's Word. His marriage to Jezebel, a Sidonian princess, further angered YEHOVAH as Jezebel was a worshipper of Ba_l. Influenced by his wife to commit further transgressions against YEHOVAH, Ahab built a temple to Ba_l and worshipped and served the false deity rather than the Elohim of Israel.

Then, in a move to consolidate power, Jezebel ordered the death of all of YEHOVAH's prophets in order to install the prophets of Ba_l as the priestly class of Israel. It is in this setting that Elijah, one of the last remaining prophets of YEHOVAH, stood up against both Ahab and Jezebel:

> And it came to pass, when Ahab saw Elijah, that Ahab said unto him, *Art* thou he that troubleth Israel? And he answered, I have not troubled Israel; but thou, and thy father's house, in that ye have forsaken the commandments of YEHOVAH, and thou hast followed Baalim. Now therefore send, *and* gather to me all Israel unto mount Car-

> mel, and the prophets of Baal four hundred and fifty, and the prophets of the groves four hundred, which eat at Jezebel's table. So Ahab sent unto all the children of Israel, and gathered the prophets together unto mount Carmel.
>
> I KINGS 18:17-20

Once the children of Israel and the false prophets were gathered at Mount Carmel, Elijah confronted the people with the need to choose which elohim they would serve:

> And Elijah came unto all the people, and said, How long halt ye between two opinions? if YEHOVAH *be* Elohim, follow him: but if Baal, *then* follow him. And the people answered him not a word. Then said Elijah unto the people, I, *even* I only, remain a prophet of YEHOVAH; but Baal's prophets *are* four hundred and fifty men.
>
> I KINGS 18:21-22

Then, in one of the most dramatic passages in the Bible, the prophet Elijah risks his life by challenging the priests of Ba_l to a match between the true Elohim YEHOVAH and the false deity Ba_l. Rather than let

Calling on the Name

YEHOVAH's name come to *"none effect"* Elijah puts it all on the line as he lays down the rules of the match in the following verse:

> And call ye on the name of your elohim, and I will call on the name of YEHOVAH: and the elohim that answereth by fire, let him be Elohim. And all the people answered and said, It is well spoken.
> I KINGS 18:24

The showdown unfolds as two bulls are prepared for sacrifice—one by the false prophets and one by Elijah. The prophets of Ba_l were first up. After they had prepared their sacrifice they began to call on the name of Ba_l. They called on the name of their false elohim and danced for an entire morning around the altar they had built. When no fire rained down on their sacrifice Elijah began to boldly taunt them saying that perhaps their elohim was sleeping. This made the false prophets shout louder and cut themselves as was their custom. But no sign came from their elohim.

Next, Elijah beckoned the people to come closer as he began to prepare the sacrifice to YEHOVAH. First he repaired the altar of Elohim on the top of the mount that had broken down. Then he built another altar in the name of YEHOVAH from twelve stones, one stone for each tribe of Israel. After placing the bull on the new altar he instructed the people to pour water on the sacrifice and the wood. He had the people do this three times so there would be no doubt that any fire that would come down from heaven would be from a supernatural source that not even water could stop.

When evening came Elijah began to call on the name of YEHOVAH:

> And it came to pass at *the time of* the offering of the *evening* sacrifice, that Elijah the prophet came near, and said, YEHOVAH Elohim of Abraham, Isaac, and of Israel, let it be known this day that thou *art* Elohim in Israel, and *that* I *am* thy servant, and *that* I have done all these things at thy word. Hear me, O YEHOVAH, hear me, that this people may know that thou *art* YEHOVAH Elohim, and *that* thou hast turned their heart back again.
>
> I KINGS 18:36-37

Immediately after Elijah called on the name of YEHOVAH fire came down from heaven and consumed the sacrifice:

> Then the fire of YEHOVAH fell, and con-

sumed the burnt sacrifice, and the wood, and the stones, and the dust, and licked up the water that *was* in the trench. And when all the people saw *it*, they fell on their faces: and they said, YEHOVAH, he *is* the Elohim; YEHOVAH, he *is* the Elohim.
>
> I KINGS 18:38-39

Elijah commanded the people to arrest the false prophets. He had them brought down to the base of the mountain to the brook called Kishon and there he killed every one of them with a sword. If this seems harsh, remember that in the original covenant, death is the penalty for being a false prophet (Deuteronomy 13:1-5).

Elijah is not the only original covenant prophet besides Moses that called on the name of YEHOVAH. Within the books of Isaiah and Jeremiah we are exhorted to call upon the Name as well. YEHOVAH wants you to call upon His name. Elohim wants you to proclaim to the world what He has done and that His name is exalted:

> His Name is Exalted—Call Upon His Name
> And in that day shall ye say, Praise YEHOVAH, **call upon his name**, declare his doings among the people, make men-

tion that his name is exalted.

Isaiah 12:4

Be on His Right Hand—Call Upon His Name

I will take the cup of salvation, and **call upon the name** of YEHOVAH.

Psalms 116:13

Declare His Greatness—Call Upon His Name

Give thanks unto YEHOVAH, **call upon his name**, make known his deeds among the people.

I Chronicles 16:8

Know Him—Call Upon His Name

Because he hath set his love upon me, therefore will I [YEHOVAH] deliver him: I will set him on high, because he hath **known my name**. He shall **call upon me**, and I will answer him: I *will be* with him in trouble; I will deliver him, and honour him. With long life will I satisfy him, and shew him my salvation.

Psalms 91:14-16

Even when the prophets tried to hold back the voice of YEHOVAH within themselves, they could not:

> Then I said, I will not make mention of him [YEHOVAH], nor speak any more in his name. But *his word* was in mine heart as a burning fire shut up in my bones, and I was weary with forbearing, and I could not *stay*.
> JEREMIAH 20:9

This is how the Word of YEHOVAH and the name of YEHOVAH should resonate in the hearts of believers—as a burning fire within us. Regardless of how the world system attempts to marginalize Elohim and make the way to Heaven as wide as the expanse of outer space we should not let our soul become discouraged. We should rather let our hearts burn with passion for the Word of YEHOVAH and our voice proclaim His deeds and His name to all the ends of the Earth:

> Yet I [YEHOVAH] have left *me* seven thousand in Israel, all the knees which have not bowed unto Baal, and every mouth which hath not kissed him.
> I KINGS 19:18

Proclaim His Holy Name

Chapter 15

Promises in the Messiah's Name

> And in that day ye shall ask me nothing. Verily, verily, I say unto you, Whatsoever ye shall **ask the Father in my name**, he will give *it* you. Hitherto have ye asked nothing in **my name**: ask, and ye shall receive, that your joy may be full.
>
> JOHN 16:23-24

In this chapter you will learn that every heavenly promise and hope is contained within the person and name of the only Son of Elohim: Yehoshua. You will discover just how essential Yehoshua's obedience was and is to our heavenly Father:

> For thus saith the high and lofty One that inhabiteth eternity, whose name *is* Holy; **I [YEHOVAH] dwell in the high and holy place**, with him [Messiah] also *that is* of

> **a contrite and humble spirit**, to revive the spirit of the humble, and to revive the heart of the contrite ones.
>
> ISAIAH 57:15

All the promises within the Messiah were pre-ordained by our heavenly Father thousands of years before Yehoshua's birth. Yehoshua is the fulfillment of over 365 original covenant scriptures spoken forth by YEHOVAH's anointed kings, prophets, and even by Moses. Just as Moses was a miracle-working prophet, a deliverer from bondage, and a mediator between YEHOVAH and man, so too is our saviour Yehoshua. Moses prophesied the following about Yehoshua:

> YEHOVAH thy Elohim will raise up unto thee a Prophet from the midst of thee, of thy brethren, like unto me; unto him ye shall hearken; According to all that thou desiredst of YEHOVAH thy Elohim in Horeb in the day of the assembly, saying, Let me not hear again the voice of YEHOVAH my Elohim, neither let me see this great fire any more, that I die not. And YEHOVAH said unto me, They have well *spoken that which they have spoken*. I will raise them up a Prophet from among their brethren,

like unto thee, and will put my words in his mouth; and he shall speak unto them all that I shall command him.

DEUTERONOMY 18:15-18

The prophet spoken of by Moses is the Messiah, the Son of YEHOVAH, and his full name is "Yehoshua ben YEHOVAH" (since he was conceived by the Holy Spirit of YEHOVAH). However, he was probably identified by the people in his hometown of Nazareth as *Yehoshua bar Yosef bar Ya'akov*, (bar is Aramaic for "son of") which when translated into English becomes Joshua, son of Joseph, son of Jacob. It is very unlikely that he was called "Jesus Christ" by anyone who knew him personally; and rather than being his last name, "Christ" is actually the English version of the Greek word *Christos*, which means "*the anointed one.*" The Hebrew primitive root word for "anointed" is *mashach*, which means "*to spread.*" To be anointed by YEHOVAH is to be filled with and consecrated by the Holy Spirit:

> And the messenger answering said to her, 'The Holy Spirit shall come upon thee, and the power of the Highest shall overshadow thee, therefore also the holy-begotten thing

shall be called Son of Elohim;
LUKE 1:35 (YLT)

Biblical records declare that the Messiah was conceived by the Holy Spirit and born to the virgin Mary and her husband Joseph over 2000 years ago in Bethlehem, the town of King David's birth (Matthew 2:1, Luke 2:4-11).

Scholars disagree as to the exact year of Yehoshua's birth. In general it is believed to have been between 4-6 B.C.[1] since multiple sources validate that King Herod died in 4 B.C. and scripture shows that Yehoshua was born near the end of Herod's reign.

Within Judaism there have been many prophets, priests, and kings who were anointed by Elohim's Holy Spirit to bring His will into manifestation on the Earth. However, there is only one begotten Son of Elohim and he is known as "The Anointed One." Traditionally the Jewish people know "The Anointed One" as the Messiah. He is their anointed King who will deliver them from their enemies, reestablish them as a nation on their permanent Elohim-given promised land, rule over them and keep them in perfect safety and peace, in "*shalom.*" Shalom in Hebrew means more than *peace* (the absence of war); it actually means "*nothing missing, nothing broken.*"

Unfortunately, most Jewish people have rejected Yehoshua as Ha Mashiach (the Messiah) because their "traditions of men" have blinded them to the truth. Additionally, some rabbis counsel their people *to not* read certain sections from the book of Isaiah (chapters 52-57) that clearly reveal how Yehoshua met the messianic scriptural requirements. In fact, it has been calculated that the odds of one person fulfilling just eight of the 365 original covenant messianic prophecies is one in $10^{17\text{th}}$ power![2]

While this is not a book about how Yehoshua has fulfilled all these prophecies, suffice it to say that Bible-familiar believers today are well aware that end-time events (such as Israel becoming a nation again in 1948) are unfolding rapidly to where the conditions heralding the return of Yehoshua as reigning King have nearly all been met.

In recognition of his brethren's rejection, Yehoshua himself said:

> But Yehoshua said unto them, A prophet is not without honour, but in his own country, and among his own kin, and in his own house.
>
> MARK 6:4

King and High Priest

As we have presented throughout this book, understanding the meaning of Hebrew names and their primitive roots is central to uncovering the depth and the rich entirety of what is promised to the believer. Let's take a look now at Yehoshua's various names and titles, keeping in mind the fact that Hebrew names not only define a person as an individual, but they also define and contain his character, his reputation, and his destiny within the will of YEHOVAH.

Hearkening to Yehoshua's role as future King, many biblical references also give him the name *Yehoshua ben David* since his lineage is traced to King David from the tribe of Judah (II Samuel 7:12-16; Psalms 132:11; Matthew 1:6-16):

> Behold, the days come, saith YEHOVAH, that I will raise unto David a righteous Branch, and a **King** shall reign and prosper, and shall execute judgment and justice in the earth. In his days Judah shall be saved, and Israel shall dwell safely: and this *is* his **name** whereby he shall be called, YEHOVAH OUR RIGHTEOUSNESS.
>
> JEREMIAH 23:5-6

Promises in the Messiah's Name

The role of a King has traditionally been to protect, rule over, and care for the people within his Kingdom. Messiah Yehoshua, as King of Heaven and future reigning King on Earth, has been given by our heavenly Father the title, "YEHOVAH OUR RIGHTEOUSNESS." In this role he reigns over us on behalf of our Elohim, and he must be sinless and of perfect moral character. Although he was tempted by Satan just as we are, he remained a Torah-observant Jew who was found pleasing to YEHOVAH:

> While he yet spake, behold, a bright cloud overshadowed them: and behold a voice out of the cloud, which said, This is my beloved Son, in whom I am well pleased; hear ye him.
>
> MATTHEW 17:5

The Hebrew root word for righteousness is *tzedek* which means *"to walk in a straight line."* Synonyms for it include: truthful, holy, pure, and virtuous. This means that Yehoshua, as King, completely met YEHOVAH's requirement of ethical conduct, particularly as it relates to his fulfillment of YEHOVAH's will on Earth and his relationship with humanity. Yehoshua is our *righteous* protector, our *righteous* saviour, our *righteous* deliverer who gave his life for us.

In fact, when we are born again Yehoshua's righteousness becomes ours and we can approach the Father with no fear of judgement for our sins were borne by Yehoshua on the cross and will be remembered no more (Jeremiah 31:31-34). Yehoshua, our righteousness, keeps us in perfect peace and safety. He is the perfect representation of his Father (in Word, in actions, in character, and will) for he does only what YEHOVAH tells him:

> And I know his commands lead to eternal life; so I say whatever the Father tells me to say.
> JOHN 12:50 (NLT)

Because the virtues that are within YEHOVAH are also found in His Son, a great many titles and qualities have been ascribed to and prophesied about Yehoshua:

> For unto us a child is born, unto us a son is given: and the government shall be upon his shoulder: and his name shall be called Wonderful, Counseller, The mighty El, The everlasting Father, The Prince of Peace. Of the increase of *his* government and peace *there shall be* no end, upon the throne of

> David, and upon his kingdom, to order it, and to establish it with judgment and with justice from henceforth even for ever. The zeal of YEHOVAH of hosts will perform this.
>
> ISAIAH 9:6-7

In addition to his role as King of Heaven and Earth, Yehoshua Ha Mashiach was anointed by the Holy Spirit to fulfill the role of the ultimate prophet of YEHOVAH. While the typical dictionary usually defines a prophet as *"one whose words are divinely inspired by G_d,"* within Judaism the meaning is taken to a deeper level. To the children of Israel, the prophets have traditionally represented Elohim among the people. They were His mouthpiece ever since the time of Moses when they, out of fear, requested that YEHOVAH not speak to them directly. Through the prophets' actions and spoken words, YEHOVAH accomplishes His will on Earth. Yehoshua, as the Son of YEHOVAH, *is* the embodiment and very essence of the WORD of Elohim:

> And the Word was made flesh, and dwelt among us, (and we beheld his glory, the glory as of the only begotten of the Father,) full of grace and truth.
>
> JOHN 1:14

In addition to serving as King and Prophet for YEHOVAH, Yehoshua also fulfills the role of eternal High Priest. You might be wondering how this could be since Yehoshua's lineage is traced from the tribe of Judah, in the line of King David. To understand this, one must first examine the Levitical priesthood and how it was a shadow picture of things to come.

First of all, the Levite priesthood was based on human lineage, originating with Aaron, the first High Priest. This means that within Judaic law only those descended from Aaron, of the tribe of Levi, could serve as priests of Israel. Each priest had a specific function within the priesthood. The traditional role of the Levitical High Priest was to make the atoning sacrifices for his own sins, the sins of his household, and for the sins of the Jewish nation (once a year on Yom Kippur). These blood sacrifices had to be done over and over again, year after year, because they only *covered* sin, they did not *take away* sin. The blood sacrifices were a shadow picture, a preparation for the *eternal* salvation that was accomplished by Yehoshua's blood sacrifice on the cross.

Yehoshua's role as eternal High Priest comes from the line of Melchizedek. You might be wondering: Who was Melchizedek and why is he important? Melchizedek was the *only priest* of YEHOVAH who was *also a king*:

Promises in the Messiah's Name

> And Melchizedek **king** of Salem brought forth bread and wine: and he *was* the **priest** of the most high Elohim. And he blessed him, and said, Blessed *be* Abram of the most high Elohim, possessor of heaven and earth: And blessed be the most high Elohim, which hath delivered thine enemies into thy hand. And he gave him tithes of all.
>
> GENESIS 14:18-20

Melchizedek's name means *"King of Righteousness and Peace."* He was the King of Salem (Jerusalem), the holy city where YEHOVAH put His name. Melchizedek was the priest of YEHOVAH long before the Levitical priesthood was established in the time of Moses. Through the line of Melchizedek, who was both King and Priest, Yehoshua's appointment as eternal High Priest was divinely ordained by his Father YEHOVAH:

> And being made perfect, he became the author of eternal salvation unto all them that obey him; Called of Elohim an high priest after the order of Melchizedec.
>
> HEBREWS 5:9-10

The Levitical priesthood only covered the sins of the Jewish nation while the Melchizedek priesthood through Messiah Yehoshua offers eternal redemption for Jews as well as all the nations of the world. Thus we can see that Yehoshua is the *fulfillment* of the original covenant's sacrificial system in his role as the perfect lamb of YEHOVAH who bore the sin (iniquity, lawlessness) of the whole world. He is the eternal and only High Priest: Mediator for all mankind:

> These things have I written unto you that believe on the **name** of the Son of Elohim; that ye may know that ye have **eternal life**, and that ye may believe on the **name** of the Son of Elohim.
> I JOHN 5:13

In the verse above notice that John took special care to assure us that eternal life is a promise for all who believe on the name of Yehoshua. However, eternal life is a subject that few want to discuss or even think about in this modern era. Today the focus is on getting a quick fix for any suffering we are experiencing and grasping at as much "happiness" as we can in this present life because anything else is "unknowable" and therefore a waste of time.

However, like it or not, as sure as you were born

into this life, you will be exiting it. It is just a matter of time. Perhaps it will be fifty years from now when you are old; or perhaps it could be tonight. Regardless of WHEN, unless you are raptured like Enoch and Elijah, your body *will* die and return to the earth—but it is up to you where the real you, your spirit, will go. Believe it or not, your destination won't be determined by an "angry" Elohim. *Your* choice, *your* free will, determines your eternal destination. Through Yehoshua, whose name means "YEHOVAH is Salvation," you have been given a choice: the choice to live forever through him, or to die in your sin. In a nutshell the following verse contains the greatest promise ever made in Yehoshua's name:

> But these are written, that ye might believe that Yehoshua is the Messiah, the Son of Elohim; and that believing **ye might have life through his name**.
>
> JOHN 20:31

And again, what is his name? It is YEHO-SHUA. When you call on and speak out the name of Yehoshua, you are actually proclaiming: YEHOVAH IS SALVATION! Some scholars translate his name even more personally, into: "YEHOVAH is my SALVATION!" The Hebrew primitive root word for salvation is the verb "yasha," which means *"to deliver, save, set free, and to comfort"* and it is descriptive of not only Yehoshua's *being* but also his *actions*.

Yehoshua's actions fulfilled YEHOVAH's salvation promise by ushering in the new covenant that was foreshadowed by the prophet Jeremiah:

> Behold, the days come, saith YEHOVAH, that I will make a new covenant with the house of Israel, and with the house of Judah: Not according to the covenant that I made with their fathers in the day *that* I took them by the hand to bring them out of the land of Egypt; which my covenant they brake, although I was an husband unto them, saith YEHOVAH: But this *shall be* the covenant that I will make with the house of Israel; After those days, saith YEHOVAH, I will put my law in their inward parts, and write it in their hearts; and will be their Elohim, and they shall be my people. And they shall teach no more every man his neighbour, and every man his brother, saying, Know YEHOVAH: for they shall all know me, from the least of them unto the greatest of them, saith YEHOVAH: for I will forgive

their iniquity, and I will remember their sin no more.

JEREMIAH 31:31-34

Isn't this promise amazing? *"I will forgive their iniquity, and I will remember their sin no more."* How is this possible? It is only possible through a redemptive sacrifice of blood—the blood of Yehoshua, who is the only intercessor between mankind and YEHOVAH, for all power and authority are declared in his holy name:

> Wherefore Elohim also hath highly exalted him, and given him a **name** which is above every name: That at the **name** of Yehoshua every knee should bow, of *things* in heaven, and *things* in earth, and *things* under the earth; And *that* every tongue should confess that Yehoshua the Messiah *is* Master, to the glory of Elohim the Father.
>
> PHILIPPIANS 2:9-11

The Word states that YEHOVAH has placed *everything* in Heaven and *everything* on Earth under the jurisdiction of Yehoshua. Don't be deluded by those who say, "Don't worry, there are many paths that lead to Heaven; only narrow-minded fundamentalists believe Yehoshua is the only way." Also, don't fall for new age delusions such as, "I'm sure the Creator will know and honor the fact that I am a sincere seeker as I dutifully repeat my secret mantras over and over again, awaiting enlightenment." If you are looking for ETERNAL LIFE IN HEAVEN there is only one name that will save you:

> Neither is there **salvation** in any other: for there is none other **name** [Yehoshua] under heaven given among men, whereby we must be saved.
>
> ACTS 4:12

Many may comfort themselves in the belief that just by being a "good" person they or their loved ones will have life everlasting in Heaven. It may make them feel better to believe this, but it is not scripture. For we have all sinned and come short, and the truth is that we are saved by grace through faith in Yehoshua, not by works (Ephesians 2:8-9).

We cannot save ourselves. Our hard work, our holiness, our fasting, our worldly reputation, our name, cannot save us from eternal damnation. If our good works alone could redeem us from our sins then Yehoshua's sacrifice and death on the cross would have been in vain (of none effect).

Yehoshua said himself, *"Enter ye in at the strait*

gate: for wide is the gate, and broad is the way, that leadeth to destruction..." (Matthew 7:13). The key that unlocks the narrow entry gate for mankind is belief and trust in *one* name: Yehoshua, who is the living Word of YEHOVAH. Believe with your heart and confess Yehoshua with your mouth. Death and life are in the power of the tongue (Proverbs 18:21)! If you confess *someone else* with your tongue (spoken words), do you think the Father will honor this promise of salvation? Yehoshua is the way, the truth, and the life. No one comes to the Father but through him and his redemptive sacrifice:

> If ye abide in me, and my words abide in you, ye shall ask what ye will, and it shall be done unto you. Herein is my Father glorified, that ye bear much fruit; so shall ye be my disciples. As the Father hath loved me, so have I loved you: continue ye in my love. If ye keep my commandments, ye shall abide in my love; even as I have kept my Father's commandments, and abide in his love. These things have I spoken unto you, that my joy might remain in you, and *that* your joy might be full.
>
> JOHN 15:7-11

Yehoshua came to Earth to reconcile us with our Creator; to show us who *our* Father is, that we might *know* Him—for every word he spoke, every healing mercy he granted, every miracle he performed, was given to him to do by our Father in Heaven. By deepening your relationship with Yehoshua and confessing him by his name, you will learn how to "walk a straight line" *with* him—you will be *tzedek* (righteous). This glorifies YEHOVAH and leads you into salvation.

Most people, when they think upon the promise contained in the word "salvation," think of it primarily as the *"forgiveness of sins unto life eternal."* However, within the richness of the original Greek (root: *sozo*) and Hebrew (root: *yasha*) the word *salvation* contains a more complete promise: of perfect safety, soundness, deliverance, preservation, prosperity, redemption, sanctification, and healing.

How do we manifest Messiah's full promise within the Word (of healing, for example) in our lives? It is through the baptism of the Holy Spirit, wherein we are "born again" in the Holy Spirit and from that birth we are given the power to manifest the gifts of the Holy Spirit:

> But the Comforter, *which is* the Holy Ghost, whom the Father will send **in my name**, he shall teach you all things, and bring all

things to your remembrance, whatsoever I
have said unto you.

JOHN 14:26

What does Yehoshua say that the Holy Ghost will do for you, a believer? He will teach you ALL things. Not just a couple of things. ALL THINGS. Let's look at these promises in Messiah's name:

> He that believeth and is baptized shall be saved; but he that believeth not shall be damned. And these signs shall follow them that believe; **In my name** shall they cast out devils; they shall speak with new tongues; They shall take up serpents; and if they drink any deadly thing, it shall not hurt them; they shall lay hands on the sick, and **they shall recover**.
>
> MARK 16:16-18

Maybe you're wondering: "What is this baptism of the Holy Spirit?" Perhaps you were baptized in water when you were a baby, like Peter and Linda were. That water baptism is not the baptism of the Holy Spirit; rather it is the baptism of repentance which represents the washing away of one's sins, and it should probably occur when one is old enough to understand it. We were not taught about the baptism of the Holy Spirit within the Catholic Church. However, we had heard about certain denominations where people "spoke in tongues" but we did not know why they did it nor did we know that it is a manifestation of the Holy Spirit. We thought it was strange, "out there," and unnecessary.

As it says in Hosea 4:6 "*My people are destroyed for lack of knowledge,*" and we have found this to be true. While we have always been hungry for Elohim, our search was mostly unfruitful until we received the baptism of the Holy Spirit. The Holy Spirit opened the eyes of our understanding; to the Word, to the importance of speaking in tongues, to the reality that healing is not just a rare miracle for a few lucky saints—rather it is promised to every believer who has accepted Yehoshua as their King and Saviour.

Even though Yehoshua came originally to save the lost house of Israel, this special baptism of the Holy Spirit is not just for the Jew:

> Behold my servant, whom I have chosen; my beloved, in whom my soul is well pleased: I will put my spirit upon him, and he shall shew judgment to the Gentiles...
> **And in his name** shall the Gentiles trust.
> MATTHEW 12:18, 21

So don't hesitate, seek and receive the baptism of the Holy Spirit (Acts 2:38-39) and your relationship with Elohim will deepen. The signs and wonders Yehoshua spoke of in Mark 16 will follow you. Yes, this *is* for you. It doesn't matter what has held you back in the past nor what you believe is preventing you from receiving in the present: YEHOVAH sent Yehoshua to heal us all. To heal and deliver us from *all* of our infirmities and diseases; this includes the healing of mental and emotional conditions such as depression:

> The Spirit of YEHOVAH *is* upon me, because he hath anointed me to preach the gospel to the poor; **he hath sent me to heal the brokenhearted**, to preach deliverance to the captives [of sin/Satan], and recovering of sight to the blind, to set at liberty them that are bruised,
>
> LUKE 4:18

There is no condition that Yehoshua refused to heal. Think about this. Meditate upon how he brought life back into Lazarus after he had been dead for four days. Before he raised him from the dead, Lazarus' brain had been without oxygen for four days; his heart had not pumped blood for four days; his body had been rotting in the heat for four days (see John 11:39).

THERE IS NOTHING THAT CAN STOP THIS HEALING POWER, except unbelief, self-righteousness, and the lack of knowledge and trust in the Word.

Perhaps you are like many sincere people who have thought, "I have prayed for years for healing, but it hasn't worked. I don't know why G_d won't answer my prayers." Here is how to receive from the King: First, we must believe with our whole heart in Yehoshua as the Son of YEHOVAH. We must call upon his name and confess it with our lips—that he is our Saviour and our life-source. Then we must renew our mind in the Holy Word (the Gospels of MATTHEW, MARK, LUKE, AND JOHN are a good place to begin). The Gospels should be as familiar to us as what is commonly called the "Lord's prayer" (Luke 11:2, Matthew 6:9). Remember that Yehoshua told us that his words are like living water (John 4:10, 6:63):

> It is the spirit that quickeneth; the flesh profiteth nothing: the words that I speak unto you, *they* are spirit, and *they* are life.
> JOHN 6:63

His Word has been given to believers as the source of life and spirit. The Messiah promises that if you renew your mind in the Word then your life will be refreshed with the living water of the spirit and the gifts and the power of the Holy Spirit of YEHOVAH will reside within you.

What does this mean? It means that as Yehoshua did, so too it is promised to you to do, for the glory of YEHOVAH. Remember Luke 11:13:

> If ye then, being evil, know how to give good gifts unto your children: how much more shall *your* heavenly Father give the Holy Spirit to them that ask him?
>
> LUKE 11:13

The Gift of the Holy Spirit

Do you want the healing promised to you by the Messiah? You can have it, because Yehoshua "healed them all" (Matthew 8:16, 12:15, 15:30; Mark 6:56). Whatever sickness may be coming against you, it is included in "them all." It does not matter that 2000 years have passed since Yehoshua walked the Earth, healing is available for all, even those "afar off," who believe on his name:

> Then Peter said unto them, Repent, and be baptized every one of you in the name of Yehoshua the Messiah for the remission of

sins, and ye shall receive the gift of the Holy Ghost. For the promise is unto you, and to your children, and **to all that are afar off**, *even* as many as YEHOVAH our Elohim shall call.

Acts 2:38-39

In the verses above the apostle Peter demonstrated how early followers of Yehoshua received the Holy Spirit. This is the same baptism that is available for you today, because you have believed in Yehoshua, in his name, without having seen him:

> Yehoshua saith unto him, Thomas, because thou hast seen me, thou hast believed: **blessed *are* they that have not seen, and *yet* have believed**.
>
> John 20:29

Yehoshua has placed this special blessing upon you, the far-off believer, who trusts in him and abides in him, because you believe on his *name*, which contains the full promise of all that is within the will of YEHOVAH:

> And whatsoever ye shall ask **in my name**, that will I do, that the Father may be glori-

fied in the Son.

JOHN 14:13

If you look closely at Yehoshua's words in John 14:13, you will see that whatever you ask of him (that is within the will of YEHOVAH as revealed in the scriptures) is yours, including the power to cast out the devil. Yes *you can* cast out the devil for although Satan is the author of sin and sickness, Yehoshua defeated him once and for all 2000 years ago and has returned back to mankind the authority over the world that was lost by Adam:

> He that committeth sin is of the devil; for the devil sinneth from the beginning. For this purpose the Son of Elohim was manifested, that he might destroy the works of the devil.
>
> I JOHN 3:8

Even though Satan is defeated, he does not want modern man to know that. He is still trying to lead us into sin, into addiction, into hopelessness, into despair and away from the will of the Father. But believers do not need to fear this, for they can do what Yehoshua did if they accept and receive the power and authority that is promised within the baptism of the Holy Spirit:

> Behold, I give unto you power to tread on serpents and scorpions, and **over all [ALL] the power of the enemy**: and nothing shall by any means hurt you.
>
> LUKE 10:19

and:

> When the even was come, they brought unto him many that were possessed with devils: and **he cast out the spirits with *his* word, and healed all that were sick**: That it might be fulfilled which was spoken by Esaias the prophet, saying, himself took our infirmities, and bare *our* sicknesses.
>
> MATTHEW 8:16-17

Healing the sick, like Yehoshua did, often involved casting out the spirits (devils) that caused the disease or infirmity. For example:

> And, behold, there was a woman which had a **spirit of infirmity** eighteen years, and was bowed together, and could in no wise lift up *herself.* And when Yehoshua saw her, he called *her to him*, and said unto

> her, Woman, thou art loosed from thine infirmity. And he laid *his* hands on her: and immediately she was made straight, and glorified Elohim.
>
> LUKE 13:11-13

Yehoshua has promised us that born-again believers can command the same kind of physical, emotional, and mental healings into manifestation that he did. This means that within the born-again believer lies the power to give sight to the blind; to make the deaf hear; and even to raise the dead back into life (Luke 7:22):

> Then they took away the stone *from the place* where the dead was laid. And Yehoshua lifted up *his* eyes, and said, Father, I thank thee that thou hast heard me. And I knew that thou hearest me always: but because of the people which stand by I said *it*, that they may believe that thou hast sent me. And when he thus had spoken, he cried with a loud voice, Lazarus, come forth. And he that was dead came forth, bound hand and foot with graveclothes: and his face was bound about with a napkin. Yehoshua saith unto them, Loose him,

and let him go.

JOHN 11:41-44

As unimaginable as this "raising from the dead power" seems to be in this scientific and faithless age, there are some fairly recent cases of people who have raised others from the dead by the power of the Holy Spirit.[3]

Not only have believers been given the power to heal and to raise the dead, they have also been given the power to transform the elements with their words—in Yehoshua's name they too can rebuke the wind and the waves:

> And he [Yehoshua] arose, and rebuked the wind, and said unto the sea, Peace, be still. And the wind ceased, and there was a great calm.
>
> MARK 4:39

If we believe and do not doubt in our heart then we can manifest even more of his promise: we can transform water into wine (John 2:4-11), we can multiply the loaves (Matthew 14:19-21), and we can tell our "mountain" where to move (Matthew 21:21):

> Yehoshua answered and said unto them,

> Verily I say unto you, If ye have faith, and doubt not, ye shall not only do this *which is done* to the fig tree, but also if ye shall say unto this mountain, Be thou removed, and be thou cast into the sea; it shall be done.
>
> MATTHEW 21:21

The Messiah promises that his very presence will be with us when we gather together in his name:

> Verily I say unto you, Whatsoever ye shall bind on earth shall be bound in heaven: and whatsoever ye shall loose on earth shall be loosed in heaven. Again I say unto you, That if two of you shall agree on earth as touching any thing that they shall ask, it shall be done for them of my Father which is in heaven. For where two or three are gathered together **in my name, there am I in the midst of them**.
>
> MATTHEW 18:18-20

As Yehoshua's word becomes alive in your heart through renewing your mind in Bible study and as you learn to trust in his promises, you will begin to operate in the gifts of the Holy Spirit. The many gifts of the Spirit, as identified by the Apostle Paul, are as follows:

> But the manifestation of the Spirit is given to every man to profit withal. For to one is given by the Spirit the **word of wisdom**; to another the **word of knowledge** by the same Spirit; To another **faith** by the same Spirit; to another the **gifts of healing** by the same Spirit; To another the **working of miracles**; to another **prophecy**; to another **discerning of spirits**; to another ***divers kinds of tongues***; to another the **interpretation of tongues**:
> I CORINTHIANS 12:7-10

And if this were not enough, the Messiah also promises the following:

> Verily, verily, I say unto you, He that believeth on me, **the works that I do shall he do also; and greater *works* than these shall he do**; because I go unto my Father.
> JOHN 14:12

The nature of these "greater works" we can only imagine. The possible immensity of them is hinted at by the disciple John (the one whom Yehoshua loved—see John 20:2) when he wrote:

Promises in the Messiah's Name

> And there are also many other things which Yehoshua did, the which, if they should be written every one, I suppose that even the world itself could not contain the books that should be written. Amen.
>
> JOHN 21:25

The blessings and promises of the Messiah are many and diverse; and they are *all* within our reach, if we will only seek him with our whole heart, trust in him, rely upon him, and do not doubt when we CALL UPON HIS NAME:

> I [Yehoshua] know thy works: behold, I have set before thee an open door, and no man can shut it: for thou hast a little strength, and hast kept my word, and hast not denied **my name**.
>
> REVELATION 3:8

Proclaim His Holy Name

Chapter 16

Your Name in Eternity

> Fear not: for I *am* with thee: I will bring thy seed from the east, and gather thee from the west; I will say to the north, Give up; and to the south, Keep not back: bring my sons from far, and my daughters from the ends of the earth; *Even* every one that is called by my name: for I have created him for my glory, I have formed him; yea, I have made him.
>
> Isaiah 43:5-7

Throughout this book we have shown you scripture from both the original and the new covenant that demonstrate Elohim's desire for His holy name to be known, honored, and glorified by us—His creation. However, this last chapter focuses not as much on YEHOVAH's name but more on you and where *your name* will be found in eternity—for eternity is where you will be spending the overwhelming majority of your existence.

For some people eternity is so vast a concept that they feel that there is no point in even thinking about it. They just shrug their shoulders and go about their daily life as if it's a given that their place in eternity is secure. For others, eternity and the concept of life after death is only a fantasy concocted by weak-minded men and women. But the prophet Isaiah says otherwise:

> Thy dead *men* shall live, *together with* my dead body shall they arise. Awake and sing, ye that dwell in dust: for thy dew *is as* the dew of herbs, and the earth shall cast out the dead.
> ISAIAH 26:19

Even though most people believe that there is life after death they spend more time accumulating material wealth rather than securing their place in eternity. The fallen nature of man and the influence of Satan in this world have pushed humanity into a myopic view of reality that is carnally based. Yehoshua warned us of this short-sightedness in the following parable:

> And he spake a parable unto them, saying, The ground of a certain rich man brought

forth plentifully: And he thought within himself, saying, What shall I do, because I have no room where to bestow my fruits? And he said, This will I do: I will pull down my barns, and build greater; and there will I bestow all my fruits and my goods. And I will say to my soul, Soul, thou hast much goods laid up for many years; take thine ease, eat, drink, *and* be merry. But Elohim said unto him, *Thou* fool, this night thy soul shall be required of thee: then whose shall those things be, which thou hast provided? So *is* he that layeth up treasure for himself, and is not rich toward Elohim.

LUKE 12:16-21

What does it mean to be "rich" toward Elohim? The Greek word translated as "rich" in Luke 12:21 is *ploutōn* which means *"to be rich."* However the root of the word is believed to have originated from the Greek word *pleó* that means *"to flow, abound."* So the verse could be translated as:

> So *is* he that **stores** up treasure for himself,
> and does not **flow toward** Elohim.
>
> LUKE 12:21

The Messiah also teaches us another lesson related to the fruits of our labor (our treasure) in the Gospel of Matthew:

> Lay not up for yourselves treasures upon earth, where moth and rust doth corrupt, and where thieves break through and steal: But lay up for yourselves treasures in heaven, where neither moth nor rust doth corrupt, and where thieves do not break through nor steal: For where your treasure is, there will your heart be also.
>
> MATTHEW 6:19-21

Elohim has promised to multiply our blessings yet He can't multiply anything on our behalf if we have invested zero in His Kingdom. This is seen in the following passage from the Gospel of Luke:

> Give, and it shall be given unto you; good measure, pressed down, and shaken together, and running over, shall men give into your bosom. For with the same measure that ye mete withal it shall be measured to you again.
>
> LUKE 6:38

Where will you be throughout eternity?

Consider that the first five books of the Bible, the Torah, speak nothing directly about an afterlife. When a Biblical personality died in the original covenant the scriptures do not say whether they were taken to Heaven or to Hell but rather usually states that the person *"was gathered to his people."*

> Then Abraham gave up the ghost, and died in a good old age, an old man, and full *of years*; and was gathered to his people.
> GENESIS 25:8

To complicate the issue even more consider what YEHOVAH says to Adam as part of the effect of Adam's eating from the tree of the knowledge of good and evil:

> In the sweat of thy face shalt thou eat bread, till thou return unto the ground; for out of it wast thou taken: for dust thou *art*, and **unto dust shalt thou return**.
> GENESIS 3:19

So which is it? Are we *"gathered unto our people"*—to our ancestors that have gone before us—or do we become as dust? The answer is both, for both concepts are contained in the Word. We can reconcile these two concepts by understanding that man is composed of three essential parts as follows:

<u>1. The Body</u>—this is the part of us that is simply flesh. It is the part that will return to dust when our days on this Earth come to a close.

<u>2. The Soul</u>—this is the part of us that is our personality. It can be considered our mind and emotions; our likes and dislikes; our way of looking at life.

<u>3. The Spirit</u>—this is the eternal never-ending self that will exist in eternity—either in union with Elohim or in eternal separation from Him in the lake of fire.

Two of the three parts of man are clearly seen while the third is hidden. The first part, the body, is what we can plainly see in a mirror. It has physical needs such as air, water, and food to exist.

The second part, the soul, is made apparent to us by the thoughts and feelings that we experience each day. However, your thoughts and feelings are not you for you can actually watch the thoughts that your mind is thinking and monitor the emotions that you are experiencing. In fact, you can even rebuke negative thoughts and override destructive emotions.

The third part of you—the real you—the eternal part, the Spirit, is hidden from obvious view. However, even though it is hidden from view, the attributes of a born-again Spirit can be known by reading and meditating on the Word of Elohim for the Word of Elohim is the mirror which reflects back to us who we are in the Spirit.

Yehoshua taught that we cannot enter into the kingdom of Heaven without being born again in the Spirit. In this *second* birth, the Spirit of Elohim begins to reside in us, and our spirit self is re-created—it becomes perfected. Now with a reborn Spirit, the Word becomes alive to us and we can understand it and live in harmony with it as it was intended.

How can we be sure that we have an everlasting spirit? According to Genesis 1:27 mankind was created in the image of YEHOVAH, therefore we can understand more about ourselves by learning what the Word says about YEHOVAH. Here is a short list of attributes of Elohim that are also found in us:

YEHOVAH has desires

We have been created in the image of Elohim—therefore as Elohim has desires we also have desires:

> For I [YEHOVAH] **desired** mercy, and not sacrifice; and the knowledge of Elohim more than burnt offerings.
>
> HOSEA 6:6

YEHOVAH has emotions

We have been created in the image of Elohim—therefore as Elohim has emotion we also have emotion:

> And it repented YEHOVAH that he had made man on the earth, and it **grieved** him at his heart.
>
> GENESIS 6:6

YEHOVAH is Spirit

We have been created in the image of Elohim—therefore as Elohim's Spirit exists our spirit exists:

> Elohim *is* a Spirit: and they that worship him must worship *him* in **spirit** and in truth.
>
> JOHN 4:24

The reason that the Torah does not speak directly about an afterlife is clear when you consider that the Torah contains shadow pictures of things to come. The Torah deals with this physical life while the new covenant goes deeper, past this outward life to the innermost heart of the Law and to the spiritual reality of Heaven.

The Exodus of the children of Israel out of Egypt under the leadership of Moses is a shadow picture of mankind being led out of the bondage of sin by the Messiah. This is seen in the story of the Passover. The Passover lamb that was sacrificed by each family and whose blood covered their doorposts delivered them from the death angel.

Likewise, Yehoshua, the sinless lamb of Elohim, sacrificed his life to release us from the slavery of Satan. His blood washes away the sin and disease of the world.

By accepting the sacrifice of Yehoshua we are, in essence, covering the doorposts of our heart with his blood. Just as the death angel passed over the Israelites who had covered their doorposts with the blood of the Passover lamb, so too are we freed from the curse of death and receive the promise of eternal life. This is because we have accepted Messiah Yehoshua into our hearts and have covered ourselves with the blood of the Lamb of Elohim. This is the exceedingly good news of the Gospel.

The Promised Land

YEHOVAH promised Abraham that his seed (the children of Israel) would inhabit a land flowing with milk and honey—the promised land. Yet when the people were at the promised land's door the vast majority of them were afraid to enter it. Why? Because there were many walled cities and strong warriors (giants) occupying the land (Numbers 13:32-33). The children of Israel let their fear override their trust in YEHOVAH's Word.

If the Passover Exodus from Egypt is a shadow picture of redemption then what are we to make of the forty years spent by the Israelites wandering in the wilderness? A whole generation was sentenced to live out their lives in the desert, never to enter the promised land because of their unbelief in the Word of Elohim. What is this a shadow picture of?

The prophetic picture for believers today is that Yehoshua is the guide to *our* promised land—the Kingdom of Heaven. We have been promised eternal life if we believe in him. If we believe in him we are "to do" his commandments—the will of the Father (John 14:15). Sadly, today's parallel to the lost generation of Israelites who did not trust in YEHOVAH when they were at the promised land's door could be what Yehoshua spoke of in Matthew chapter 7:21-23:

> Not every one that saith unto me, Master, Master shall enter into the kingdom of heaven; **but he that doeth the will of my Father** which is in heaven. Many will say to me in that day, Master, Master have we not prophesied in thy name? and in thy name have cast out devils? and in thy name done many wonderful works? And then will I profess unto them, I never knew you: depart from me, ye that work iniquity.
>
> MATTHEW 7:21-23

As explained elsewhere in this book, "iniquity" is running one's life by one's own set of rules (self-righteousness) rather than running one's life according to the Righteousness of YEHOVAH (the Father's will). And how can one tell who is the ruler of their life—Satan or YEHOVAH? By the two verses that are written directly before Yehoshua's warning above:

> Every tree that bringeth not forth good fruit is hewn down, and cast into the fire. Wherefore **by their fruits ye shall know them**.
>
> MATTHEW 7:19-20

While our actions alone cannot gain us acceptance into Heaven, they do produce "fruit." The "fruit" we produce can be used to measure the state of our relationship with the Father and the Son. But what of the fruit that was claimed by those people Yehoshua spoke of in Matthew 7:21-23? Wasn't that "good" fruit? No, it was counterfeit "fruit." The counterfeit fruit is grown from man's vanity. While it may look good on the outside it is rotten on the inside. The *real* fruit is based on the seed of the Word of Elohim planted in your heart that changes your life in a supernatural way.

In the same way that our actions alone do not gain us eternal life, just saying that we believe in Yehoshua doesn't either. For even demons believe in Yehoshua (that Yehoshua exists and he is the Son of Elohim—Mark 1:23-24). The apparent disconnect here comes from a lack of understanding of what it means to "*believe.*" Yehoshua said that if we believe in him, truly and continually, then signs that prove this fact will follow:

> And these signs shall follow them that **believe**; In my name shall they cast out devils; they shall speak with new tongues; They shall take up serpents; and if they drink any deadly thing, it shall not hurt them; they shall lay hands on the sick, and

they shall recover.

MARK 16:17-18

The word "believe" in the verse above is from the Greek *pisteuó* which also can mean to *"trust in"* or *"adhere to."* So another way of translating the passage is: "And these signs shall follow them that *trust in my name"*—the name Yehoshua.

What does it mean to trust someone? The Israelites who were condemned to wander in the wilderness until their generation had all died did not trust in YEHOVAH, in other words when push came to shove they truly did not believe Him—that He would help them to defeat the inhabitants of the land thus fulfilling His promise. They treated their relationship with Elohim similar to how Isaiah described the children of Israel hundreds of years later:

> Wherefore Elohim said, Forasmuch as this people draw near *me* with their mouth, and with their lips do honor me, but have removed their heart far from me, and their fear toward me is taught by the precept of men:
>
> ISAIAH 29:13

Similarly we should not only say we *believe* in

Yehoshua, but rather we must have a direct knowledge of and relationship with him as well as place our *trust* in him. If we trust in him, and we love him, we will do his commandments—for which of us would desire to turn our backs on the Kingdom of Heaven as did the lost generation of Israel who turned away from the promised land because of their unbelief in the promises and power of YEHOVAH? Let us have FAITH in Elohim!

The manner in which we conduct our life on Earth is an outward reflection of the state of our relationship with Yehoshua. If we truly trust (believe) in Yehoshua and follow his commands we will strengthen our relationship with him—he will "know" us and therefore our life will bear good fruit because of what has been planted in our hearts. Our life will not produce counterfeit fruit as those referred to by Yehoshua in Matthew 7:21-23 whose lips honor YEHOVAH but their hearts are far from Him. Those who produce good "fruit" love the name of YEHOVAH:

> Yea, in the way of thy judgments, O YEHOVAH, have we waited for thee; the desire of *our* soul *is* to thy name, and to the remembrance of thee.
>
> ISAIAH 26:8

Just as we honor YEHOVAH's name with a pure heart, YEHOVAH has created two special books with which to honor us. These two books are referred to within the pages of the Bible as "The Books of Elohim." They are: 1) The Book of Life, and 2) The Book of Remembrance. Both of these books are important in determining where your name will be for eternity.

References to the "Book of Life" are found in both the original and the new covenant. In the original covenant the prophet Daniel writes about end-time survivors—the ones whose names are written in Elohim's book:

> And at that time stand up doth Michael, the great head, who is standing up for the sons of thy people [Israel], and there hath been a time of distress, such as hath not been since there hath been a nation till that time, and at that time do thy people escape, every one who is found **written in the book**.
>
> DANIEL 12:1 (YLT)

In the book of Exodus both YEHOVAH and Moses refer to a book that is most likely the "Book of Life." In the following verse Moses is appealing to Elohim to be merciful to the children of Israel who have sinned against YEHOVAH by worshipping a golden calf at the base of Mount Sinai:

> Yet now, if thou [YEHOVAH] wilt forgive their sin—; and if not, blot me, I pray thee, out of **thy book** which thou hast written.
> EXODUS 32:32

Moses appears to be offering himself as a sacrifice for the sins of the children of Israel but YEHOVAH makes it clear to Moses that He *will* blot out the names of those who sin against Him out of His book (the Book of Life) and *will not* accept Moses as a replacement:

> And YEHOVAH said unto Moses, Whosoever hath sinned against me, him will I blot out of **my book**.
> EXODUS 32:33

The new covenant also speaks of the "Book of Life." In the book of Revelation we find a promise from the Messiah that our names will not be taken from the "Book of Life" if we are found worthy:

> Thou hast a few names even in Sardis which have not defiled their garments; and they shall walk with me in white: for they

are worthy. He that overcometh, the same shall be clothed in white raiment; and I [Yehoshua] will not blot out his **name** out of the **book of life**, but I will confess his **name** before my Father, and before his angels.

REVELATION 3:4-5

In these verses our worth is measured by the fact that we have not "defiled our garments." Defile means *"to make unclean or impure."* Of course Yehoshua is not talking about the physical clothes one wears. The garment spoken of could be considered a "covering." The believer's covering is Yehoshua, i.e., it is his blood that covers their sin. Therefore, for our names to be left intact in the Book of Life we must keep our relationship with Yehoshua (our covering) from being polluted by unbelief or the traditions of men. Resist the devil and he will flee (James 4:7).

It is written that after the last judgment has occurred YEHOVAH will create a new Jerusalem. It will be a glorious city filled with never-ending light and the eternal presence of Elohim. This new city will descend directly from Heaven to the Earth and only those written in the Book of Life will be allowed to enter its gates to fellowship with Elohim and the Messiah as seen in the following verses:

> And I saw no temple therein: for Adonai El Shaddai and the Lamb are the temple of it. And the city [New Jerusalem] had no need of the sun, neither of the moon, to shine in it: for the glory of Elohim did lighten it, and the Lamb *is* the light thereof. And the nations of them which are saved shall walk in the light of it: and the kings of the earth do bring their glory and honour into it. And the gates of it shall not be shut at all by day: for there shall be no night there. And they shall bring the glory and honour of the nations into it. And there shall in no wise enter into it any thing that defileth, neither *whatsoever* worketh abomination, or *maketh* a lie: but they which are written in the Lamb's **book of life**.
>
> REVELATION 21:22-27

How important is it that your name will be found in the Book of Life? Consider the following verses from the book of Revelation that show that on the last great day, when all are to be judged, YEHOVAH's books, including the Book of Life, will be opened and His righteous judgment will be executed:

> And I [John] saw the dead, small and great,

stand before Elohim; and the books were opened: and another book was opened, which is *the book* of life: and the dead were judged out of those things which were written in the books, according to their works. And the sea gave up the dead which were in it; and death and hell delivered up the dead which were in them: and they were judged every man according to their works. And death and hell were cast into the lake of fire. This is the second death. And whosoever was not found written in **the book of life** was cast into the lake of fire.

Revelation 20:12-15

In the passage above we see that the judgment of man is based on information in the 'other' books and not from the Book of Life itself. These 'other' books contain the deeds of men, good deeds and bad deeds. In other words it doesn't matter how many good or bad deeds you may have written in these 'other' books—if your name is not written in the Book of Life you will be cast into the lake of fire.

How does your name get into the Lamb's Book of Life? It is not by our righteousness that we are saved and our name written in the Book of Life but it is through our accepting of the blood sacrifice of

YEHOVAH's sinless Son. It is through this sacrifice and a relationship with Yehoshua that our names are written in the Book of Life (not by our own deeds should any man boast). Therefore, for your name to be written in the Book of Life you need a personal relationship with the Messiah and you need to confess him (profess your faith and trust in him) before men and women:

> Whosoever therefore shall confess me before men, him will I confess also before my Father which is in heaven.
> MATTHEW 10:32

You also need to have the second birth (John 3:3-8, Acts 2:38) where you will receive the gift of the Holy Spirit. You will then begin to speak with new tongues, cast out devils, and heal the sick by the laying on of hands—as a true disciple of Yehoshua.

You need to follow Yehoshua's commandments—to *love* YEHOVAH with your whole heart, mind, and soul, and *love* your neighbor as yourself (Matthew 22:37-39). Instead of following your own will in this world you need to do the Father's will.

The second special book written of in the Bible is the "Book of Remembrance." Does YEHOVAH forget? No, Elohim does not forget. The word "remembrance" is not used here as the common meaning of forgetting something and then remembering it. Rather it is used here as a memorial—a memorial with your name in it. The scriptures state that if you fear YEHOVAH, i.e., *have profound adoring awed respect for* Him and His name then you too can have a page in this special book of Elohim:

> Then they that feared YEHOVAH spake often one to another: and YEHOVAH hearkened, **and heard *it***, and a **book of remembrance** was written before him for them that feared YEHOVAH, and that thought upon his **name**.
> MALACHI 3:16

Do you want to be remembered by YEHOVAH? When the last judgment day is upon us will you then be able to plead your case? Lay up treasures in Heaven now. Cultivate a relationship with Yehoshua now. Get to know him and the Father by meditating on the Word. Invite the Holy Spirit into your heart now. Honor the great and glorious name of Elohim now by focusing on His name with all your heart and mind and soul and then your name will be placed in YEHOVAH's special Book of Remembrance.

Throughout this book we have presented scriptures that reveal YEHOVAH's desire for His name to be known, spoken, glorified, and honored by us—His creation. Our special prayer and blessing for you is that you come to know YEHOVAH, the one true Elohim, and His only Son, our Redeemer, our brother in Spirit: Yehoshua (John 20:17, Mark 3:35).

We pray that the living Spirit of YEHOVAH be born within you. We pray that your name will be found in the Book of Life and in the Book of Remembrance. May you honor YEHOVAH by proclaiming His holy name and may you live in eternal union with Elohim, His Son Yehoshua, the Holy Spirit, the heavenly host, and all the saints who worship YEHOVAH in Spirit and in Truth.

> I have remembered thy name, O YEHOVAH, in the night [when no man could see], and have kept thy law [instructions].
>
> PSALMS 119:55

How to Receive Salvation and Eternal Life

Elohim has given all his of us a *way* back into right relationship with Him again—as it was in the beginning in the Garden of Eden before mankind sinned and forfeited their birthright to Satan. This *way* is through repenting (turning away) from sin and accepting the blood sacrifice of His only begotten Son Yehoshua for the Bible states that without the shedding of blood there is no remission of sin.

Yehoshua's blood was shed for your sin; past, present, and future on the cross at Calvary 2000 years ago. But just as the Israelites had to place the blood of the passover lamb on their doorposts in Egypt so that the destroyer would 'pass-over' their homes (saving alive all inside), you must place the blood of Yehoshua, the perfect spotless unblemished Lamb of Elohim, upon the doorposts of your heart. If you do so then the penalty for your sin will 'pass-over' you for you are made righteous by the blood of the Lamb:

> ...for I [YEHOVAH] will forgive their iniquity, and I will remember their sin no more.
> JEREMIAH 31:34

If you have not accepted this free gift of salvation through the blood sacrifice of Yehoshua, or if you are not sure if you have truly accepted Yehoshua the Messiah as your Master and you want to be saved and have a relationship with him and with Elohim then pray this prayer (out loud) from your heart:

Dear Father Yehovah,

Thank you for your Word, for it says that all who call upon your name YEHOVAH shall be saved (Joel 2:32, Romans 10:13); and that "All that the Father giveth me shall come to me; and him that cometh to me I will in no wise cast out (John 6:37)."

I want to know You and be with You and Yehoshua forever. I repent and turn away from sin. I trust and believe with all my heart that Yehoshua the Messiah is Your only begotten Son, and that his death on the cross paid the penalty for my sin (John 3:16). I believe that you raised your Son Yehoshua from the dead. I confess with my mouth and believe with all my heart that he is the way, the truth, and the life and no one comes to You except through him (John 14:6). I accept the free gift of Salvation right now in the name of Yehoshua.

With my whole heart I commit my life to You, and with my mouth I confess before all that Your Son Yehoshua is my Master and Saviour. I believe that I am now a new creation in him and that I live through him. Amen.

Signed _____ Date: _____

Salvation and Eternal Life

Introducing

The Proclaim His Holy Name Bible
King James Version

Enhanced Red Letter Edition
With the Father and the Son's words in red and Their Hebrew names restored

Paperback, 9.25 x 7.5, 938 pages

About the Proclaim His Holy Name Bible

The *Proclaim His Holy Name Bible, with the Father and the Son's words in red*, has been published to honor and glorify our Creator, YEHOVAH, the Mighty One of Israel, the King of the universe and His holy son Yehoshua (Jesus) our Redeemer, our Messiah and our High Priest. Within its pages the Creator's words are highlighted in red and His actual name is restored to its rightful place within the scriptures. The Messiah's words are highlighted in red and his actual Hebrew name Yehoshua is restored to the scriptures as well. While many Bibles have been published with the Messiah's words in red, this is the first version of the Bible that has the Father's spoken words in red as well. In the Gospel of John the Messiah told us that he only did what the Father told him to do. Therefore, if the Son's words are highlighted in red it is appropriate to do so for the Father's words as well.

> "And I know that his commandment is life ever-lasting: whatsoever I speak therefore, even as the Father said unto me, so I speak."
>
> JOHN 12:50

Key Highlights of the Proclaim His Holy Name Bible

At last you can own a Bible with both the Father and the Son's words both in red and with both the Father and the Son's true names restored! The *Proclaim His Holy Name Bible* will lead you to a greater awareness and appreciation for the Father's name: YEHOVAH, and show you how famous Biblical personalities including the Creator Himself proclaimed His holy name. It will bless you and inspire to proclaim His holy name! Key highlights of the *Proclaim His Holy Name Bible* are as follows:

- The Father's true name YEHOVAH is restored!
- The Messiah's Hebrew name Yehoshua is restored!
- Words of the Father and Son are highlighted in red.
- Words of the Father or the Son that are recounted by a biblical personality or an angel are highlighted in blue.
- Key verses related to the Name are highlighted with a special background color to assist the reader in his/her studies.
- Includes 23 full color maps depicting various locales and activities associated with the books of the Bible.

The text of the Proclaim His Holy Name Bible is taken word for word from the public domain King James version of the Holy Bible. However, there are some changes that have been made as noted here:

1. The Creator's Name has been restored
The phrase 'the LORD' has been changed to YEHOVAH, the actual name of Elohim as found throughout the original Hebrew text.

2. The Creator's Name in Italics
In many places in the King James version you will see words in italics. These words are not found in the original Hebrew text but were rather added by the King James translators. There are a few interesting italics additions where the Creator's name is shown in italics as 'the LORD' (see Ex. 33:9). We have replaced this with YEHOVAH in italics.

3. The Messiah's name has been restored
Jesus' Hebrew name has been restored in this volume as Yehoshua. While some refer to Jesus as Yeshua, Yahshua, and other such versions we believe his proper name to be Yehoshua.

Salvation and Eternal Life

4. Upper case 'Lord' has been changed to Adonai in the Old Testament

The word 'Lord' has suspect origins most likely coming from the word 'Ba_l,' the name of a pagan deity (we have omitted a letter from these pagan deities names to honor YEHOVAH's command to not let the name of other elohim be mentioned, see Ex. 23:13). Therefore the upper case word 'Lord' used to refer to the Creator has been changed to the Hebrew word Adonai as found in the original scriptures. In other cases it has been changed to King or Master depending on context.

5. Upper case 'Lord' changed to YEHOVAH or Master in the New Testament

Because of the ambiguity of the translation from Greek to English with the use of simply 'the Lord' (without 'Lord' being in all caps as 'LORD'), the line between references to the Father and to the Son is blurred. We have done our best when changing the word 'Lord' to either a reference to YEHOVAH, or to 'Master' when referring to the Messiah throughout the New Testament text. Other words replaced for 'Lord' in this edition are Adoni, Ruler, Adonai, and Elohim as context dictates.

6. The lower case word 'lord' has been changed to master

Due to the same issues with the suspect origins of the word 'Lord' the lower case 'lord' has been removed from this edition. It has predominately been changed to master. Other changes for 'lord' may be husband, ruler, and noble as context dictates.

7. The upper case word G_d has been replaced with Elohim

Because the English word G_d is derived from questionable pagan origins we chose to replace it with the Hebrew word pronounced El-o-him instead. The Hebrew word Elohim is found throughout the original Hebrew scriptures. We have replaced references to the one G_d with upper case Elohim for the same reasons as explained above. The word G_dhead has been changed to Divine or Divine Nature. G_dly has been changed to Holy or Elohim-like. G_d-ward has been changed to "towards Elohim."

8. The lower case word g_d has been replaced with elohim

For reasons explained above the lower case words g_d and g_ds (plural) have been changed to elohim. Also g_dly has been changed to holy, and ung_dly to unholy.

9. Almighty G_d has been changed to El Shaddai

The Hebrew title El Shaddai has replaced G_d Almighty. Once again, because of the suspect origins of the word 'G_d' we have opted to use the original Hebrew title.

10. Christ has been changed to Messiah

The Hebrew term Messiah replaces the Greek word Christ throughout this New Testament volume. The full title and name 'The Lord Jesus Christ' has been changed to 'The Master Yehoshua the Messiah.'

11. E_ster has been changed to Passover

E_ster is the English translation of the name of a pagan deity. The word 'E_ster' has been changed to Passover as found in the original scriptures.

The *Proclaim His Holy Name Bible* is available at online booksellers everywhere. For more information on our books please visit: www.onlyBelievePublishing.com.

Proclaim His Holy Name Ministries

Proclaim His Holy Name Ministries is dedicated to proclaiming and promoting the Father's name YEHOVAH, preaching the full Gospel (Good News) of the Bible, and leading people to salvation through the redemptive power of the blood of the Father's only begotten Son Yehoshua (Jesus).

For more information regarding the holy names of the Father and the Son please visit the Proclaim His Holy Name ministries website at:

www.ProclaimHisHolyName.org

On the site you will find articles, books, videos, and other information to assist you in your studies on the Name and the Holy Bible.

Shalom

Appendices

Proclaim His Holy Name

Appendix A

THE CREATOR PROCLAIMED HIS OWN NAME

And YEHOVAH descended in the cloud, and stood with him there, and proclaimed the name of YEHOVAH.

EXODUS 34:5

YEHOVAH's will for His holy name to be known and proclaimed has been made clear. He Himself stated His name explicitly over 70 times in the Torah (the first five books of the Bible) alone as shown in the table below (bold emphasis added):

Gen 15:7	And he said unto him, **I *am* YEHOVAH** that brought thee out of Ur of the Chaldees, to give thee this land to inherit it.
Gen 28:13	And, behold, YEHOVAH stood above it, and said, **I *am* YEHOVAH** Elohim of Abraham thy father, and the Elohim of Isaac: the land whereon thou liest, to thee will I give it, and to thy seed;

Ex 6:2-3	And Elohim spake unto Moses, and said unto him, **I am YEHOVAH**: And I appeared unto Abraham, unto Isaac, and unto Jacob, by *the name of* El Shaddai but by **my name YEHOVAH** was I not known to them.
Ex 6:6	Wherefore say unto the children of Israel, **I *am* YEHOVAH**, and I will bring you out from under the burdens of the Egyptians, and I will rid you out of their bondage, and I will redeem you with a stretched out arm, and with great judgments:
Ex 6:7	And I will take you to me for a people, and I will be to you an Elohim: and ye shall know that **I *am* YEHOVAH** your Elohim, which bringeth you out from under the burdens of the Egyptians.
Ex 6:8	And I will bring you in unto the land, concerning the which I did swear to give it to Abraham, to Isaac, and to Jacob; and I will give it you for an heritage: **I *am* YEHOVAH**.
Ex 6:29	That YEHOVAH spake unto Moses, saying, **I *am* YEHOVAH**: speak thou unto Pharaoh king of Egypt all that I say unto thee.
Ex 7:5	And the Egyptians shall know that **I *am* YEHOVAH**, when I stretch forth mine hand upon Egypt, and bring out the children of Israel from among them.
Ex 7:17	Thus saith YEHOVAH, In this thou shalt know that **I *am* YEHOVAH**: behold, I will smite with the rod that *is* in mine hand upon the waters which *are* in the river, and they shall be turned to blood.
Ex 8:22	And I will sever in that day the land of Goshen, in which my people dwell, that no swarms *of flies* shall be there; to the end thou mayest know that **I *am* YEHOVAH** in the midst of the earth.

The Creator Proclaimed His Own Name

Ex 10:2	And that thou mayest tell in the ears of thy son, and of thy son's son, what things I have wrought in Egypt, and my signs which I have done among them; that ye may know how that **I am YEHOVAH**.
Ex 12:12	For I will pass through the land of Egypt this night, and will smite all the firstborn in the land of Egypt, both man and beast; and against all the elohim of Egypt I will execute judgment: **I am YEHOVAH.**
Ex 14:4	And I will harden Pharaoh's heart, that he shall follow after them; and I will be honoured upon Pharaoh, and upon all his host; that the Egyptians may know that **I am YEHOVAH**. And they did so.
Ex 14:18	And the Egyptians shall know that **I am YEHOVAH**, when I have gotten me honour upon Pharaoh, upon his chariots, and upon his horsemen.
Ex 15:26	And said, If thou wilt diligently hearken to the voice of YEHOVAH thy Elohim, and wilt do that which is right in his sight, and wilt give ear to his commandments, and keep all his statutes, I will put none of these diseases upon thee, which I have brought upon the Egyptians: for **I am YEHOVAH** that healeth thee.
Ex 16:12	I have heard the murmurings of the children of Israel: speak unto them, saying, At even ye shall eat flesh, and in the morning ye shall be filled with bread; and ye shall know that **I am YEHOVAH** your Elohim.
Ex 20:2-3	**I am YEHOVAH** thy Elohim, which have brought thee out of the land of Egypt, out of the house of bondage. Thou shalt have no other elohim before me.

Ex 29:46	And they shall know that **I am YEHOVAH** their Elohim, that brought them forth out of the land of Egypt, that I may dwell among them: **I am YEHOVAH** their Elohim.
Ex 31:13	Speak thou also unto the children of Israel, saying, Verily my sabbaths ye shall keep: for it *is* a sign between me and you throughout your generations; that *ye* may know that **I am YEHOVAH** that doth sanctify you.
Lev 11:44	For **I am YEHOVAH** your Elohim: ye shall therefore sanctify yourselves, and ye shall be holy; for I *am* holy: neither shall ye defile yourselves with any manner of creeping thing that creepeth upon the earth.
Lev 11:45	For **I am YEHOVAH** that bringeth you up out of the land of Egypt, to be your Elohim: ye shall therefore be holy, for I *am* holy.
Lev 18:2	Speak unto the children of Israel, and say unto them, **I am YEHOVAH** your Elohim.
Lev 18:4	Ye shall do my judgments, and keep mine ordinances, to walk therein: **I am YEHOVAH** your Elohim.
Lev 18:5	Ye shall therefore keep my statutes, and my judgments: which if a man do, he shall live in them: **I am YEHOVAH**.
Lev 18:6	None of you shall approach to any that is near of kin to him, to uncover *their* nakedness: **I am YEHOVAH**.
Lev 18:21	And thou shalt not let any of thy seed pass through *the fire* to Molech, neither shalt thou profane the name of thy Elohim: **I am YEHOVAH**.

Lev 19:3	Ye shall fear every man his mother, and his father, and keep my sabbaths: **I *am* YEHOVAH** your Elohim.
Lev 19:4	Turn ye not unto idols, nor make to yourselves molten elohim: **I *am* YEHOVAH** your Elohim.
Lev 19:10	And thou shalt not glean thy vineyard, neither shalt thou gather *every* grape of thy vineyard; thou shalt leave them for the poor and stranger: **I *am* YEHOVAH** your Elohim.
Lev 19:12	And ye shall not swear by my name falsely, neither shalt thou profane the name of thy Elohim: **I *am* YEHOVAH**.
Lev 19:14	Thou shalt not curse the deaf, nor put a stumblingblock before the blind, but shalt fear thy Elohim: **I *am* YEHOVAH**.
Lev 19:16	Thou shalt not go up and down *as* a talebearer among thy people: neither shalt thou stand against the blood of thy neighbour: **I *am* YEHOVAH**.
Lev 19:18	Thou shalt not avenge, nor bear any grudge against the children of thy people, but thou shalt love thy neighbour as thyself: **I *am* YEHOVAH**.
Lev 19:25	And in the fifth year shall ye eat of the fruit thereof, that it may yield unto you the increase thereof: **I *am* YEHOVAH** your Elohim.
Lev 19:28	Ye shall not make any cuttings in your flesh for the dead, nor print any marks upon you: **I *am* YEHOVAH**.
Lev 19:30	Ye shall keep my sabbaths, and reverence my sanctuary: **I *am* YEHOVAH**.

Lev 19:31	Regard not them that have familiar spirits, neither seek after wizards, to be defiled by them: **I am YEHOVAH** your Elohim.
Lev 19:32	Thou shalt rise up before the hoary head, and honour the face of the old man, and fear thy Elohim: **I am YEHOVAH**.
Lev 19:34	*But* the stranger that dwelleth with you shall be unto you as one born among you, and thou shalt love him as thyself; for ye were strangers in the land of Egypt: **I am YEHOVAH** your Elohim.
Lev 19:36	Just balances, just weights, a just ephah, and a just hin, shall ye have: **I am YEHOVAH** your Elohim, which brought you out of the land of Egypt.
Lev 19:37	Therefore shall ye observe all my statutes, and all my judgments, and do them: **I am YEHOVAH**.
Lev 20:7	Sanctify yourselves therefore, and be ye holy: for **I am YEHOVAH** your Elohim.
Lev 20:8	And ye shall keep my statutes, and do them: **I am YEHOVAH** which sanctify you.
Lev 20:24	But I have said unto you, Ye shall inherit their land, and I will give it unto you to possess it, a land that floweth with milk and honey: **I am YEHOVAH** your Elohim, which have separated you from *other* people.
Lev 21:12	Neither shall he go out of the sanctuary, nor profane the sanctuary of his Elohim; for the crown of the anointing oil of his Elohim *is* upon him: **I am YEHOVAH**.

Lev 22:2	Speak unto Aaron and to his sons, that they separate themselves from the holy things of the children of Israel, and that they profane not my holy name *in those things* which they hallow unto me: **I *am* YEHOVAH**.
Lev 22:3	Say unto them, Whosoever *he be* of all your seed among your generations, that goeth unto the holy things, which the children of Israel hallow unto YEHOVAH, having his uncleanness upon him, that soul shall be cut off from my presence: **I *am* YEHOVAH**.
Lev 22:8	That which dieth of itself, or is torn *with beasts*, he shall not eat to defile himself therewith: **I *am* YEHOVAH**.
Lev 22:30	On the same day it shall be eaten up; ye shall leave none of it until the morrow: **I *am* YEHOVAH**.
Lev 22:31	Therefore shall ye keep my commandments, and do them: **I *am* YEHOVAH**.
Lev 22:32	Neither shall ye profane my holy name; but I will be hallowed among the children of Israel: **I *am* YEHOVAH** which hallow you,
Lev 22:33	That brought you out of the land of Egypt, to be your Elohim: **I *am* YEHOVAH**.
Lev 23:22	And when ye reap the harvest of your land, thou shalt not make clean riddance of the corners of thy field when thou reapest, neither shalt thou gather any gleaning of thy harvest: thou shalt leave them unto the poor, and to the stranger: **I *am* YEHOVAH** your Elohim.

Lev 23:43	That your generations may know that I made the children of Israel to dwell in booths, when I brought them out of the land of Egypt: **I am YEHOVAH** your Elohim.
Lev 24:22	Ye shall have one manner of law, as well for the stranger, as for one of your own country: for **I am YEHOVAH** your Elohim.
Lev 25:17	Ye shall not therefore oppress one another; but thou shalt fear thy Elohim: for **I am YEHOVAH** your Elohim.
Lev 25:38	**I am YEHOVAH** your Elohim, which brought you forth out of the land of Egypt, to give you the land of Canaan, *and* to be your Elohim.
Lev 25:55	For unto me the children of Israel *are* servants; they *are* my servants whom I brought forth out of the land of Egypt: **I am YEHOVAH** your Elohim.
Lev 26:1	Ye shall make you no idols nor graven image, neither rear you up a standing image, neither shall ye set up *any* image of stone in your land, to bow down unto it: for **I am YEHOVAH** your Elohim.
Lev 26:2	Ye shall keep my sabbaths, and reverence my sanctuary: **I am YEHOVAH**.
Lev 26:13	**I am YEHOVAH** your Elohim, which brought you forth out of the land of Egypt, that ye should not be their bondmen; and I have broken the bands of your yoke, and made you go upright.
Lev 26:44	And yet for all that, when they be in the land of their enemies, I will not cast them away, neither will I abhor them, to destroy them utterly, and to break my covenant with them: for **I am YEHOVAH** their Elohim.

The Creator Proclaimed His Own Name

Lev 26:45	But I will for their sakes remember the covenant of their ancestors, whom I brought forth out of the land of Egypt in the sight of the heathen, that I might be their Elohim: **I am YEHOVAH**.
Num 3:13	Because all the firstborn *are* mine; *for* on the day that I smote all the firstborn in the land of Egypt I hallowed unto me all the firstborn in Israel, both man and beast: mine shall they be: **I am YEHOVAH**.
Num 3:41	And thou shalt take the Levites for me (**I am YEHOVAH**) instead of all the firstborn among the children of Israel; and the cattle of the Levites instead of all the firstlings among the cattle of the children of Israel.
Num 3:45	Take the Levites instead of all the firstborn among the children of Israel, and the cattle of the Levites instead of their cattle; and the Levites shall be mine: **I am YEHOVAH**.
Num 10:10	Also in the day of your gladness, and in your solemn days, and in the beginnings of your months, ye shall blow with the trumpets over your burnt offerings, and over the sacrifices of your peace offerings; that they may be to you for a memorial before your Elohim: **I am YEHOVAH** your Elohim.
Num 15:41	**I am YEHOVAH** your Elohim, which brought you out of the land of Egypt, to be your Elohim: **I am YEHOVAH** your Elohim.
Deut 5:6	**I am YEHOVAH** thy Elohim, which brought thee out of the land of Egypt, from the house of bondage.

Deut 5: 9-10	Thou shalt not bow down thyself unto them, nor serve them: for **I YEHOVAH** thy Elohim *am* a jealous Elohim, visiting the iniquity of the fathers upon the children unto the third and fourth *generation* of them that hate me, And shewing mercy unto thousands of them that love me and keep my commandments.

Appendix B

TIMELINE OF ELOHIM

> That *men* may know that thou, whose name alone *is* YEHOVAH, *art* the most high over all the earth.
>
> PSALMS 83:18

From the time of creation until the end of Moses' life there were several people that YEHOVAH spoke to, either directly or in a dream. There are also several people that the Bible specifically states "called on the name of YEHOVAH." The information in the tables below is drawn from the Torah, the five books of Moses:

People who called on the Name of YEHOVAH
(includes first occurrence only)

Person	Verse
"Men"	Genesis 4:26
Abram	Genesis 12:8
Abraham	Genesis 21:33

Person	Verse
Isaac	Genesis 26:25

People whom YEHOVAH spoke to directly or in a dream
(includes first occurrence only)

Person	Verse
"Us"	Genesis 1:26
Adam	Genesis 2:16
Eve	Genesis 3:13
Serpent	Genesis 3:14
"Us"	Genesis 3:22
Cain	Genesis 4:6
Noah	Genesis 6:13
Noah and his sons	Genesis 9:1
"Us"	Genesis 11:6-7
Abram	Genesis 12:1
Abimelech	Genesis 20:3
Rebekah	Genesis 25:23
Isaac	Genesis 26:2
Jacob	Genesis 28:13
Laban	Genesis 31:24
Moses	Exodus 3:4
The Children of Israel	Exodus 20:1
Moses & Aaron	Leviticus 13:1
Moses & Aaron & Miriam	Numbers 12:4

Balaam	Numbers 22:9
Moses & Eleazar	Numbers 26:1

Proclaim His Holy Name

Appendix C

VERSE REFERENCES BY TYPE

> Give unto YEHOVAH the glory due unto his name; worship YEHOVAH in the beauty of holiness.
>
> PSALMS 29:2

The following chart lists about 200 of the over 500 Bible verses that speak of the importance of the name of YEHOVAH as well as names in general. Many of the 500+ verses (KJV) contain both the name of YEHOVAH as well as the word "name." We've grouped the verses into one table below broken down by four categories: Key Verses, Command Verses, Blessing/Promise Verses, and Curse Verses. As you read and study these verses remember to insert His name YEHOVAH when you see the title "the LORD." For New Testament verses also consider that the word "Lord" (lower case) may actually be referring to YEHOVAH and not to Yehoshua (depending on context). The order of the books in the chart is based on Hebrew Tanakh and Greek New Testament.

Key Verses	Commands	Blessings/Promises	Curse Verses
Gen. 4:26	Ex. 23:13	Ex. 20:24	Ex. 23:21
Gen. 11:4	Lev. 18:4	Num. 6:27	Lev. 20:3
Gen. 12:2	Lev. 18:5	II Sam. 7:13	Deut. 28:58
Gen. 12:8	Lev. 18:6	I Kgs. 8:20	Deut. 29:20
Gen. 13:4	Lev. 18:21	I Kgs. 8:29	I Kgs. 9:7
Gen. 16:13	Lev. 19:12	I Kgs. 8:33	II Kgs. 2:24
Gen. 21:33	Lev. 21:6	I Kgs. 8:35	Jer. 14:15
Gen. 22:14	Lev. 22:2	I Kgs. 9:3	Jer. 25:29
Gen. 26:25	Lev. 22:32	II Kgs. 14:27	Jer. 29:21
Ex. 3:15	Lev. 24:16	Isa. 45:3	Jer. 29:22
Ex. 6:3	Lev. 24:22	Isa. 48:9	Mal. 1:14
Ex. 9:16	Deut. 5:11	Isa. 48:11	Mal. 2:2
Ex. 15:3	Deut. 6:13	Isa. 55:13	Ps. 79:6
Ex. 20:7	Deut. 10:20	Isa. 56:5	Rev. 16:9
Ex. 33:19	Deut. 12:3	Isa. 56:6-7	
Deut. 18:19	Deut. 12:4	Isa. 59:19	
Deut. 18:20	Deut. 12:5	Jer. 33:16	
I Sam. 20:42	Deut. 12:11	Jer. 50:34	
II Sam. 7:23	Deut. 12:21	Joel 2:32	

Verse References by Type

Key Verses	Commands	Blessings/ Promises	Curse Verses
I Kgs. 8:43	Deut. 14:23	Mal. 3:16	
I Kgs. 18:24	Deut. 21:5	II Chron. 6:10	
Isa. 12:4	Deut. 26:2	II Chron. 20:9	
Isa. 42:8	Josh. 23:7	Ps. 9:10	
Isa. 43:7	Josh. 23:8	Ps. 69:36	
Isa. 62:2	Nah. 1:14	Ps. 72:17	
Isa. 64:7	I Chr. 16:29	Neh. 1:9	
Jer. 10:25	Ps. 29:2	Matt. 10:22	
Jer. 16:21	Ps. 66:2	Matt. 10:41	
Jer. 20:9	Ps. 68:4	Matt. 12:21	
Jer. 23:27	Ps. 96:2	Matt. 19:29	
Ez. 20:9	Ps. 96:8	Mark 9:37	
Ez. 20:39	Ps. 100:4	Mark 9:41	
Ez. 36:21	Ps. 135:1	Mark 13:13	
Ez. 36:22	Ps. 135:3	Mark 16:17	
Ez. 39:7	Ps. 145:21	Luke 9:48	
Ez. 43:7	Matt. 28:19	John 15:16	
Ez. 43:8	Luke 24:47	John 16:23	
Mal. 1:11	Col. 3:17	John 16:24	

Key Verses	Commands	Blessings/Promises	Curse Verses
Mal. 4:2	II Thess. 3:6	Acts 2:38	
I Chr. 16:8	1 John 3:23	Heb. 6:10	
I Chr. 17:24		Rev. 3:5	
II Chr. 7:14		Rev. 3:8	
Ps. 20:7		Rev. 3:12	
Ps. 22:22		Rev. 11:18	
Ps. 45:17		Rev. 22:3	
Ps. 83:4		Rev. 22:4	
Ps. 83:18			
Ps. 106:8			
Ps. 113:3			
Ps. 140:13			
Ps. 148:13			
Prov. 22:1			
Prov. 30:4			
Eccles. 7:1			
Matt. 12:21			
Mark 9:39			
Mark 13:6			

Verse References by Type

Key Verses	Commands	Blessings/ Promises	Curse Verses
Luke 1:49			
Luke 10:17			
John 1:12			
John 3:18			
John 10:25			
John 14:13			
John 14:14			
John 14:26			
John 17:11			
John 17:12			
John 17:26			
John 20:31			
Acts 2:21			
Acts 4:12			
Acts 9:15			
Rom. 2:23-24			
Rom. 9:17			
Rom. 10:13			
Eph. 1:21			

Key Verses	Commands	Blessings/Promises	Curse Verses
Eph. 3:15			
Phil. 2:9			
Heb. 2:12			
James 5:14			
1 John 2:12			
Rev. 14:1			
Rev. 22:4			

Appendix D

Verse References by Books of the Bible

> And He [YEHOVAH] said, I will make all my goodness pass before thee, and I will proclaim the name of YEHOVAH before thee; and will be gracious to whom I will be gracious, and will shew mercy on whom I will shew mercy.
>
> Exodus 33:19

The following charts list about 200 of the over 500 Bible verses that speak of the importance of the name of YEHOVAH as well as names in general. Many of the 500+ verses (KJV) contain both the name of YEHOVAH as well as the word "name." We've grouped the verses into four separate tables: Key Verses, Command Verses, Blessing/Promise Verses, and Curse Verses. As you read and study these verses remember to insert His name YEHOVAH when you see the title "the LORD." For New Testament verses also consider that the word "Lord" (lower case) may actually be referring to YEHOVAH and not to Yehoshua (depending on context). The order of the books in each chart is based on Hebrew Tanakh and Greek New Testament.

Key Verses

Book	Verses
Genesis	4:26, 11:4, 12:2, 12:8, 13:4, 16:13, 21:33, 22:14, 26:25
Exodus	3:15, 6:3, 9:16, 15:3, 20:7, 33:19
Deuteronomy	18:19, 18:20
I Samuel	20:42
II Samuel	7:23
I Kings	8:43, 18:24
Isaiah	12:4, 42:8, 43:7, 62:2, 64:7
Jeremiah	10:25, 16:21, 20:9, 23:27
Ezekiel	20:9, 20:39, 36:21, 36:22, 39:7, 43:7, 43:8
Malachi	1:11, 4:2
I Chronicles	16:8, 17:24
II Chronicles	7:14
Psalms	20:7, 22:22, 45:17, 83:4, 83:18, 106:8, 113:3, 140:13, 148:13
Proverbs	22:1, 30:4
Ecclesiastes	7:1

Verse References by Books of the Bible

Matthew	12:21
Mark	9:39, 13:6
Luke	1:49, 10:17
John	1:12, 3:18, 10:25, 14:13, 14:14, 14:26, 17:11, 17:12, 17:26, 20:31
Acts	2:21, 4:12, 9:15
Romans	2:23-24, 9:17, 10:13
Ephesians	1:21, 3:15
Philippians	2:9
Hebrews	2:12
James	5:14
I John	2:12
Revelation	14:1, 22:4

Command Verses

Book	Verses
Exodus	23:13
Leviticus	18:4, 18:5, 18:6, 18:21, 19:12, 21:6, 22:2, 22:32, 24:14, 24:16, 24:22
Deuteronomy	5:11, 6:13, 10:20, 12:3, 12:4, 12:5, 12:11, 12:21, 14:23, 21:5, 26:2
Joshua	23:7, 23:8

Nahum	1:14
I Chronicles	16:29
Psalms	29:2, 66:2, 68:4, 96:2, 96:8, 100:4, 135:1, 135:3, 145:21
Matthew	28:19
Luke	24:47
Colossians	3:17
II Thessalonians	3:6
I John	3:23

Blessing / Promise Verses

Book	Verses
Exodus	20:24
Numbers	6:27
II Samuel	7:13
I Kings	8:20, 8:29, 8:33, 8:35, 9:3
II Kings	14:27
Isaiah	45:3, 48:9, 48:11, 55:13, 56:5, 56:6-7, 59:19
Jeremiah	33:16, 50:34
Joel	2:32

Verse References by Books of the Bible

Malachi	3:16
II Chronicles	6:10, 20:9
Psalms	9:10, 69:36, 72:17
Nehemiah	1:9
Matthew	10:22, 10:41, 12:21, 19:29
Mark	9:37, 9:41, 13:13, 16:17
Luke	9:48
John	15:16, 16:23, 16:24
Acts	2:38
Hebrews	6:10
Revelation	3:5, 3:8, 3:12, 11:18, 22:3-4

Curse Verses

Book	Verses
Exodus	23:21
Leviticus	20:3
Deuteronomy	28:58, 29:20
I Kings	9:7
II Kings	2:24

Jeremiah	14:15, 25:29, 29:21, 29:22
Malachi	1:14, 2:2
Psalms	79:6
Revelation	16:9

Appendix E

The Attributes of the Creator

> Who *is* like unto YEHOVAH our Elohim, who dwelleth on high, Who humbleth *himself* to behold *the things that are* in heaven, and in the earth!
>
> Psalms 113:5-6

The table below contains a list of attributes of YEHOVAH and His holy name that are found in the Bible. Meditate upon each of these attributes and the accompanying scriptures to grow closer to Him:

Attribute	Verses
YEHOVAH is our banner	Exodus 17:15, Psalms 20:5
YEHOVAH's name is everlasting	Isaiah 63:12, Psalms 72:17
YEHOVAH's name is glorious	Isaiah 63:14
YEHOVAH's name is mighty	Jeremiah 10:6
YEHOVAH is righteousness	Jeremiah 23:6, 33:16
YEHOVAH lives	I Kings 22:14
YEHOVAH is the redeemer	Jeremiah 50:34

Proclaim His Holy Name

Attribute	Verses
YEHOVAH's name is exalted	Isaiah 12:4
YEHOVAH is strong in power	Isaiah 40:26, Psalms 44:5
YEHOVAH is the Elohim of the whole Earth	Isaiah 54:5
YEHOVAH's name is holy	Isaiah 54:5, Psalms 97:12
YEHOVAH is our defender	Psalms 5:11
YEHOVAH's name is excellent	Psalms 8:9
YEHOVAH is trustworthy	Psalms 9:10
YEHOVAH is our judge	Psalms 54:1
YEHOVAH is most honorable	Psalms 66:2
YEHOVAH is blessed	Psalms 72:17
YEHOVAH is revered	Psalms 111:9
YEHOVAH is salvation	Psalms 116:13
YEHOVAH is our help	Psalms 124:8

Appendix F

THE GREAT DEEDS OF THE CREATOR

> The works of YEHOVAH *are* great, sought out of all them that have pleasure therein. His work *is* honourable and glorious: and his righteousness endureth for ever.
>
> PSALMS 111:2-3

We can know the greatness of the name of YEHOVAH by recounting the deeds He has done that bring Him glory and honor and that lift His holy name above all others. The table below contains a list of some of the most awesome achievements of YEHOVAH as recorded in the Bible. Also included for each achievement is a Bible verse or two for you to meditate upon. Take time to consider the power and glory of YEHOVAH as you study the verses and give praise to His holy name.

Achievement	Verse(s)
YEHOVAH created the Heavens and the Earth There are over 100 billion galaxies with over 10 billion trillion stars and there is only one planet Earth that lies in the center of Elohim's universe.	Gen. 1:1, Ps. 33:6
YEHOVAH created seed-bearing plants and vegetation There are approximately one million different seed types that auto-renew from generation to generation to provide an endless supply of food and essentials for life on Earth.	Gen. 1:11, Gen. 1:12, Gen. 1:29, Gen. 1:30, Ps. 104:14
YEHOVAH designed a perpetual watering system for the Earth All plants and vegetation were automatically watered in perfect balance.	Gen. 2:6
YEHOVAH created Man The centerpiece of Elohim's creation on Earth is man—made in Elohim's image.	Gen. 1:26, Gen. 2:7, Gen. 9:6, Ps. 8:6
YEHOVAH created birds, fish, animals, and all other living things There are over 1.2 million types of living creatures on Earth besides the centerpiece of Elohim's creation on Earth: man. Each is able to continuously reproduce and fill the Earth with its kind.	Gen. 1:20, Gen. 1:21, Gen. 1:22, Gen. 1:24, Gen. 1:25, Gen. 2:19

The Great Deeds of the Creator

Achievement	Verse(s)
YEHOVAH gave the day of rest The Sabbath day of rest for Elohim and all His creation, man and animal, has been provided. On this day man is to look towards his Creator and occupy his mind only with Him and His glory.	Gen. 2:2, Gen. 2.3, Ex. 20:8
YEHOVAH gave mankind the ability to live on Earth forever The Tree of Life was in the Garden of Eden, and mankind had access to the tree (before the fall) so that they could live forever.	Gen. 2:9, Gen. 3:22
YEHOVAH created the angels There are at least four types of angels found in the Bible: Seraphim, Cherubim, Guardian Angels, and Archangels.	Is. 6:6, Ex. 25:20 Ez. 28:16 Jude 1:9
YEHOVAH brought the Great Flood Elohim purged the Earth of all evil during the great flood to preserve an untainted blood line that would provide us our salvation in Yehoshua.	Gen. 6:17, Gen. 6:4-8
YEHOVAH opened the womb of Sarah when she was in her nineties Sarah was barren for her whole life until Elohim opened her womb to fulfill His promise to Abraham.	Gen. 21:1, Gen. 21:2, Gen. 17:21

Achievement	Verse(s)
YEHOVAH destroyed Sodom and Gomorrah These two cities were destroyed by Elohim, for like a cancer the people were totally reprobate and evil.	Gen. 19:24
YEHOVAH protected Moses from certain death All Hebrew male children from newborn to two were to be killed by order of Pharaoh yet Moses was unharmed.	Ex. 1:17, Ex. 2:5-10
YEHOVAH freed the Children of Israel from bondage in Egypt Elohim brought ten plagues against Egypt as a sign of His power to Pharaoh and to proclaim to the world the glory of Elohim's name: YEHOVAH.	Ex. 7:20, 8:5, 8:16, 8:24, 9:6, 9:10, 9:23, 10:13, 10:21, 12:12, 12:29
YEHOVAH parted the Red Sea and defeated the Armies of Pharaoh The Egyptian Army pursued the Children of Israel into the desert and was about to destroy them when Elohim ordered the Red Sea to part and swallow the pursuing Egyptian Army.	Ex. 14:28, Ex. 14:30
YEHOVAH provided food in the wilderness for over two million people Elohim gave food where there was none so that the Children of Israel could survive their journey to the promised land.	Ex. 16:15

The Great Deeds of the Creator

Achievement	Verse(s)
YEHOVAH provided water in the wilderness for over two million people Elohim gave water where there was none so that the Children of Israel could survive their years in the wilderness.	Ex. 17:6
YEHOVAH guided the Children of Israel to the promised land Elohim provided a supernatural GPS to lead Israel to the land flowing with milk and honey.	Ex. 13:21
YEHOVAH gave the ten commandments Elohim gave us instruction on how to live a holy and righteous life according to YEHOVAH's standards for mankind.	Ex. 20:1-17
YEHOVAH redeemed us from the curse of original sin YEHOVAH sent His only Son, Yehoshua, into the world so that through Their sacrifice we could have eternal life with YEHOVAH, His Son, His angels, and all the redeemed in Heaven.	John 3:14-18

Proclaim His Holy Name

Appendix G

References

Chapter 1

[1] The name of YEHOVAH is found 6828 times in the Old Testament. Source: Nehemiah Gordon from the article "The Pronunciation of the Name," available from www.karaite-korner.org/yhwh_2.pdf.

Chapter 3

[1, 2] Contraction of names was a part of an ancient practice of abbreviation. Source: Nehemiah Gordon from the article "The Pronunciation of the Name," available from www.karaite-korner.org/yhwh_2.pdf.

[3] As shown in chapter 2 of *The Lord and the Tetragrammaton* (Howard Mazzaffeo Publisher, Jan. 2011, fourth edition) by Howard Mazzaferro, YE-HO-AH means *"who shall be, who is, and who was."*

Chapter 5

[1] Source: "The Origin of the English Word for God" by Craig Bluemel, available from www.bibleanswerstand.org/God_2.htm.

[2] Source: "The Origin of the English Word for God" by Craig Bluemel, available from www.bibleanswerstand.org/God_2.htm.

[3] Source: Wikipedia, available from en.wikipedia.org/wiki/God_(word).

[4] Source: Wikipedia, available from en.wiktionary.org/wiki/egads and Dictionary.reference.com, available from www.dictionary.reference.com/

browse/egad.

Chapter 9

[1] Source: Wikipedia, available from http://en.wikipedia.org/wiki/Baal.

[2] Source: "Does Baal Gad equal the Lord God of Christianity?" by Donald Adkins, available from http://yahushua.net/baalgad.htm.

Chapter 11

[1] A jot is the 10th letter of the Hebrew alphabet (Yod) while a tittle is the small decorative spur on the upper edge of the Yod. Source: freethoughtpedia, available from freethoughtpedia.com/wiki/Old_testament_vs_new_testament.

Chapter 15

[1] While most people assume that Yehoshua was born in the year "0" neither the present Gregorian calendar nor the preceding Julian calendar included a year "0" in their calculations. Source: Wikipedia, available from en.wikipedia.org/wiki/0_(year).

[2] Source: Biblebelievers.org, "Mathematical Probability that Jesus is the Christ," available from www.biblebelievers.org.au/radio034.htm.

[3] In *Staying Full of God* (Harrison House, March 2008), by Andrew Wommack, pp.45-46, he explains how his son Peter was raised from the dead.

CPSIA information can be obtained at www.ICGtesting.com
Printed in the USA
LVOW01s0137110114

368939LV00004B/472/P